P. T. Forsyth

Per crucem ad lucem

A. M. HUNTER

SCM PRESS LTD

334 00494 2
First published 1974
by SCM Press Ltd,
56 Bloomsbury Street London
© SCM Press Ltd 1974
Printed in Great Britain by
Fletcher & Son Ltd
Norwich

P. T. Forsyth

Contents

Preface

This is an introduction to – not an exhaustive account of – the man whom Emil Brunner (who came under his influence while in England just before the First World War) called the greatest of British theologians. If it is not exhaustive, it centres on Forsyth's chief books and handles his main themes.

Since there already exist three major studies of Forsyth's theology – all by Americans – it may well be asked, why yet another one? My answer is simply that the interest in Forsyth continues unabated, that in the last decade three new books have appeared which make available to the public for the first time some valuable articles and addresses of Forsyth, and that there is room for a short book on this very remarkable Christian thinker.

Why should we read Forsyth? Let Professor Gordon Rupp answer my question: 'Forsyth's emphases are timely and modern. It seems likely that he will take his place among preachers and theologians who will be read profitably for many generations to come, not on grounds of theological anti-quarianism, but as speaking that language of the centuries which makes all Christians contemporary.'

If I may give some personal reasons why, over the years, Forsyth has been the theologian who above all others 'rang my bell', they would be these. His theology is always based four-square on the most up-to-date biblical scholarship. Hammered out in the real world and in the hurly-burly of five busy ministries, it is realistic, evangelical (in the best sense of that word) and ethical to the core. Forsyth does not lightly heal the wound of the people; he does really grapple with the final facts of human nature against which sentimental optimism is ever powerless – the facts of man's sin and guilt, as he finds God's cure for it in a great Christ and a great cross (hence my subtitle 'through cross to light'). And though sometimes provocatively polemical and often less than lucid, the man himself has a power of phrase and a gift of vivid writing which, by comparison, makes many other theologians sound trite and tame.

Robert Macafee Brown, in his excellent study of Forsyth, calls him 'prophet for today'. I should agree and argue that he is a truer one than even the mighty Barth whose excesses Forsyth avoided. We are living now in what has been called theologically 'the post-Barthian era'. The pendulum has swung back, and we are witnessing something of a return to that man-centred Christianity which Forsyth ceaselessly castigated. Yet I am content to be called a theological 'square' (along with a good many others more eminent than I) if I assert my conviction that Forsyth's theology is not only truer to the historic faith of the New Testament but much more relevantly medicative for man's spiritual sickness today than what Barth called the 'flat-tyre' version of the gospel now being peddled by our left-wing modernists in their attempt to accommodate Christianity to modern man. Once again, by reading the typescipt and helping with the proofs, my good friend, the Rev. David G. Gray (formerly of Dundee and now of Ayr), has put me deeply in his debt, and I give him my warm thanks.

A. M. Hunter

Abbreviations and Bibliography

Since Forsyth's books often have long titles, abbreviated citation of them in the notes at the end of each chapter is necessary. For those most frequently quoted, I propose the following:

GHF   *God the Holy Father*, Independent Press 1957.

PPMM   *Positive Preaching and the Modern Mind*, Hodder and Stoughton 1907.

PPJC   *The Person and Place of Jesus Christ*, Independent Press 1948.

WOC   *The Work of Christ*, Collins 1965.

POA   *The Principle of Authority*, Independent Press 1952.

JOG   *The Justification of God*, Independent Press 1957.

CEW   *The Christian Ethic of War*, Longmans, Green 1916.

C and S   *Church and Sacraments*, Longmans, Green 1917.

TLTN   *This Life and The Next*, Independent Press 1953.

CGS   *The Church, the Gospel and Society*, Independent Press 1962.

RON   *Revelation Old and New*, Independent Press 1962.

TGAA   *The Gospel and Authority* ed, M. Anderson, Augsburg 1971.

The references to *Positive Preaching and the Modern Mind* and to *Church and Sacraments* are made from the original editions. All others are from Forsyth's reprinted works.

The three major studies of Forsyth's theology are:

W. L. Bradley, *P. T. Forsyth the Man and His Work*, Independent Press 1952.

R. M. Brown, *P. T. Forsyth, Prophet for Today*, Westminster Press 1952

J. H. Rodgers, *The Theology of P. T. Forsyth*, Independent Press 1965.

In addition to these there is a short study, *The Theology of P. T. Forsyth*, by G. O. Griffith (Lutterworth Press 1948). The other contributions worth mentioning are chapter 3 of J. K. Mozley's *The Heart of the Gospel* (SPCK 1927), Harry Escott's *P. T. Forsyth, Director of Souls* (Epworth Press 1948), S. J. Mikolaski's chapter on Forsyth in *Creative Minds in Modern Theology*, ed. P. E. Hughes (Eerdmans 1966) and Jessie Forsyth Andrews' vivid memoir of her father prefixed to the reprinted edition of *The Work of Christ* (Collins 1965).

PART ONE

I

Forsyth and His Times

In a corner of the 'quad' at King's College, Old Aberdeen is a wall-plaque commemorating an alumnus member of the clan Forsyth, who spent his life as a country parson a few miles north of the Granite City. A. J. Forsyth, however, lives in history not as a preacher of the gospel but as the inventor of the percussion cap—an invention which, because he refused to sell its secret to Napoleon, earned him a pension from the British government. Five years after he died, in 1848, there was born in Aberdeen a boy with the same surname who was destined to tread the same 'quad' and later to be acclaimed 'one of the most brilliant minds in Europe' by, of all persons, the agnostic John Morley. This man has no memorial in his native city save a brief mention in the local Grammar School's roll-of-honour: 'Dux for 1864: Peter T. Forsyth.' Yet, in the opinion of Emil Brunner, he became 'the greatest of modern British theologians'. More than half a century has elapsed since his death; but the passing years, so far from diminishing his fame, have served only to increase it. All his chief books have been recently reprinted; and in the last two decades three major studies of his theology have been written by Americans.

The truth is that, like Kierkegaard, Forsyth was a great man born before his time. In an era of prosperity before two World Wars had blown sky-high the secular dogma of inevitable progress, Forsyth did what Karl Barth, Reinhold Niebuhr and others did for us in an era of collapse and despair, but with this difference: whereas they were, partly at least, commenting on accomplished facts, Forsyth was 'seeing the invisible'. Now, at long last, his *kairos* has come.

Men commonly call him 'a Barthian before Barth'. Thus, to an Irish student who had quoted Forsyth to him, Barth is said to have replied, 'If Forsyth had not said what he said when he said it, I would have said he was quoting me.' Theological likenesses between the two men there undoubtedly are. Like Barth, Forsyth steadfastly set his face against that theological temper which regards man's reason as capable of scaling the highest heights of reality. Like Barth also, Forsyth set the historic revelation in Christ at the very centre of his thinking. If Barth said, 'God loves the world. He has said Yes to mankind in Christ', Forsyth declared, 'The key to history is the historic Christ above history, and in command of it, and there is no other.'[1]

But the parallel breaks down at two crucial points: on the place of reason in revelation and on the primacy of the moral. Forsyth could never have written as the earlier Barth did. 'Faith grips reason by the throat and strangles the beast.' For Forsyth defined theology as 'faith-thinking' – the church's supernatural faith giving a reasoned account of itself. Again, whereas Barth's attitude to morality tended to be negative, Forsyth held that 'the moral is the real', and that the movements of the Supreme Being must be morally construed as they are morally revealed. Moreover, to a greater degree than Barth he appreciated the virtues of liberal theology, combining them with a christo-centric faith which is specially notable in this post-Barthian era when we are looking afresh at the virtues (as well as the vices) of nineteenth-century theology.

On all these counts some of us think Forsyth a wiser guide than Barth. Here, for example, is the personal testimony (in a letter to the writer) of an English vicar who, deeply disappointed by the lack of force and conviction in modern theology, was persuaded by that discerning judge of theology, J. K. Mozley, to dip into Forsyth: 'In Forsyth I found the strength and penetration which I needed, and when in due course I was introduced to Barth, I found myself in familiar country. But I also received the impression (which I have kept) that Forsyth was the greater because of his belief in reason, whereby he maintained the essential liberal theological principle. I also found Forsyth specially useful to one like myself, who has only worked in academic circles for a few years; for Forsyth was concerned not only with the study of the gospel, but with its *proclamation.*'

Alongside this Anglican testimony let us set that of a Scottish Presbyterian professor, Allan Galloway (he is reviewing *The Gospel and Authority, A P. T. Forsyth Reader* by the American Marvin W. Anderson): 'When one reads Forsyth in 1972, the most striking thing about him is his modernity. He anticipated much that was later developed by Karl Barth – the social and political realism of human sinfulness, the primacy of objective grace over subjective illumination, the intrinsic authority of the person of Christ, the power and finality of the Cross.'[2]

This is the just verdict of hind-sight, fifty years later. But in the 1920s and '30s Forsyth's true spiritual stature was not seen, or even glimpsed. It took another World War and its awful aftermath to send men back to the prophet of the cross and to realize that he had a real word of God for our human predicament.

First, let us say something about the life of Forsyth – enough for us to know something of his origins and spiritual pilgrimage – the place of his birth and his parentage, where he was educated, where he laboured as minister and professor, how he bore himself amid the causes and controversies of his day, the thinkers who influenced him, the figure he cut in the world, the kind of man he was.

Forsyth was born, the eldest of five children, at 100 Chapel Street, Aberdeen on 12 May 1848, and later brought up in a large rambling house in Marischal Street. His Celtic parentage may explain his remarkable gift of words – no theologian is more quotable – and the deep vein of poetry in him. His mother Elspeth Macpherson was a Highland servant lass from Kingussie who had been 'left' the big house on the death of her master Peter Taylor, a well-known citizen of Aberdeen and a staunch Congregationalist. His father, Isaac Forsyth, a weaver's son from the Cabrach hills, earned his living as a small trader and postman. A loving, spiritual, bookish man, with little of this world's goods, he had to wait, Jacob-like, nine years before he could marry his sweetheart. Then he moved into the big house, and the young couple took in boarders, mostly impecunious Highland students – among them George Macdonald, from Huntly, later to win fame as a novelist and deeply influence the thought of C. S. Lewis – who found it hard enough to pay their fees, let alone their lodgings. 'Dinna ye fash (worry),' Mrs Forsyth would say to some penniless Highland lad, 'Gin (if) ye find the siller for your fees, I'll find ye bed and bread.'

In this frugal home Forsyth grew up. At his baptism he received as Christian names those of his mother's benefactor. Yet, though very poor and never robust, his was a happy childhood spent on the banks of the Dee and Don and around the quayside of Aberdeen, then preoccupied with the harvest of the sea and with no thought of the 'black gold' beneath the sea-bed. 'I was brought up by the sea', he wrote later, 'a mile or two inland, at dead of night, when all was quiet, I used to hear the sea singing a lullaby to the fisher children on the shore beneath the moon and her family of stars.'

After schooling at Aberdeen Grammar School where, sixty years before, Lord Byron had been a pupil, he went up in the autumn of 1864 to Aberdeen University to study the classics and, like 'Shon Campbell' from Gairloch, in Mackenzie's moving ballad – 'To dive in Bain and Drew'. Alexander Bain was the eminent Aberdeen professor of Logic from whose lectures Forsyth gained an interest in Kant, Hegel and others. Eventually, he took a brilliant 'first' in classics, and for a year assisted the university professor of Latin (or, as they call it there, 'Humanity'). But, like 'Shon Campbell', 'the pulpit was his aim'; and in 1872, on the advice of his friend, William Robertson Smith, the famous Old Testament scholar, he went, for a semester, to Göttingen to sit at the feet of Albrecht Ritschl, then the lodestar for aspiring students of theology.

There he learned German and acquired a life-long interest in German theologians.

On returning to England, he entered Hackney College (now New College) London. But his health was already so fragile, and his abilities so evident, that he was allowed to leave in 1874 without completing his course. After some ten years of preparation he was about to start a career of which twenty-five years were spent in the active ministry and twenty as a professor.

Theologically, he began as an out-and-out Liberal. (Here we may stop to observe that 'Liberalism' is an ambivalent word. It represents right attitudes as well as wrong ones. In one sense, the mature Forsyth was a Liberal; in another he was not. A Liberal he was in his demand for intellectual liberty, in his insistence on the right and value of biblical criticism, in his refusal to rest content in the ancient creeds with their obsolete categories, in his concept of theology as Christian faith giving a reasoned account of revelation. The Liberalism which he early espoused, and on which he later came down like a hammer was that version of Christianity which so sought to accommodate it to the modern mind as to make shipwreck of the historic faith: which stressed evolution rather than revelation, viewed the kingdom of God as a human creation rather than a divine invasion, minimized human sin and guilt, scaled down the New Testament Christ and his cross to all-too-human dimensions, and regarded Paul as the perverter of an originally simple gospel about God's fatherhood and man's brotherhood.) From this Liberalism, as the years went by, he moved to Ritschlianism, and then, under the influence of his conversion and his study of Maurice and Dale, to a neo-orthodoxy of a very vital and evangelical kind, though wholly devoid of what he called 'pietistic wish-wash'.

In 1876 he began his ministry at Shipley, a suburb of Bradford, among the working men of Yorkshire, soon acquiring the reputation of a very unorthodox preacher in a church which the local Congregational Union refused to recognize. In 1877, the year in which he married Minna Magness, Forsyth found himself aligned with the 'radicals' against the 'conservatives' at Leicester in a theological controversy which rocked the whole denomination.

Four years later he moved from Shipley to St Thomas's Square, Hackney, London where he collected a congregation of 'heretics and suspects', shocked the primly pious by preaching in shepherd's plaid trousers, and began to take a lively interest in politics, art, music and the theatre.

When, in 1885, he entered on his third pastorate at Cheetam Hill in North Manchester, he again plunged into public life, engaged in political debate about the problems of poverty and lectured the working men on art. His interest in children, strong all his life, showed itself in the publication (with J. A. Hamilton) of a little book entitled *Pulpit Parables for Young Hearers*. Later in life, when the talk turned one day to children's hymns, and somebody admired the lines:

> I would be treated as a child
> And guided where I go,

Forsyth roguishly suggested as an improvement:

> I would be guided as a child
> And *treated* where I go.

In 1888 Forsyth moved to Clarendon Park, Leicester where for six years, besides his work as minister, he took an active part in politics and even supported the great Dock Strike of 1889. But it was in Leicester, in an essay contributed to a book called *Faith and Criticism* (1893), that he gave first proof of his coming power as a theologian. It fell under the eye of Dr Dale of Birmingham. 'Who is this P. T. Forsyth?' he said, 'He has recovered for us a word we had all but lost – the word "grace".' It was true. Preachers had come to construe this great New Testament word as the mere apotheosis of human love. Forsyth was to teach them that it means God's holy love hating sin and redeeming it in Christ's cross, and creating in the penitent sinner new life and moral amendment.

When in 1894 he moved to his last pastorate in Emmanuel Church, Cambridge, it found him in wretched health. A week after his arrival his wife died, so that for the next three or four years he lived alone with his schoolgirl daughter Jessie; and when in 1895 his *Alma Mater*, Aberdeen University made him a Doctor of Divinity, he was too weak to go north for the laureation ceremony.

Next year his famous sermon on 'the Holy Father' to the Congregational Union at Leicester made the public aware that they had to reckon with a new Forsyth. On the levity of Liberalism he had for ever turned his back; henceforth his themes were to be the holiness – the infinite majesty and utter purity – of God, the sinfulness of sin and the power of the cross by which God in Christ redeemed the world. An 'evangelical' he would be, but not in the narrow and stale sense of that word: in his hands the word 'evangel' would be moralized and revitalized.

We are so made that we do not find it easy to speak of things or events which profoundly move and change us. Forsyth was no exception. He did not speak often in any detail about his change. Nevertheless, what evidence we have suggests that the change had come some years earlier. But if his was a slow, not a sudden, conversion, it had abiding results. Once, years later, he did lift the veil a little:

There was a time when I was interested in the first degree with purely scientific criticism. Bred among academic scholarship of the classics and philosophy, I carried these habits to the Bible, and I found in the subject a huge fascination, in proportion as the stakes were much higher. But, fortunately for me, I was not condemned to the mere scholar's cloistered life. I could not treat the matter as an academic quest. I was in a relation of life, duty and responsibility to others. I could not contemplate conclusions without asking how they would affect these people and my word to them in doubt, death, grief and repentance . . . It pleased God also by the revelation of his holiness and grace, which the great theologians taught me to find in the Bible, to bring home to me my sin in a way which submerged all the school questions in weight, urgency and poignancy. I was turned from a Christian to a believer, from a lover of love to an object of grace.[3]

Ah, if only some of our spiritual mentors today would show a like sense of responsibility and could speak out of a like apprehension of the adequacy of the gospel to meet men's deepest needs! Forsyth's words remind us at once of Paul's autobiographical passages in Galatians and of Karl Barth's famous preface to his commentary on the Romans. Yet, as we have noted, though Forsyth had repudiated the errors of Liberalism (in the pejorative sense of that word), he retained all that was best in the Liberal approach to theology and the Bible. A new man in Christ, he now felt himself in his studies continually 'being corrected and humiliated by the Holy Spirit'. Later, he was to speak mordantly of those scholars who had been his first love – many of them German professors reared in pious German manses. Their fault, as he diagnosed it, was not lack of scholarly technique, but ignorance of *real life* outside the cloister or quadrangle. 'Their world,' he said, and his words have not lost their force today, 'is a study of still life; it has not the drama, the fury, the pang, the tragedy, the crisis of the actual world at large, with its horrible sin and guilt.'[4] Through his work in the ministry, where he had met men and women up against life in all its stern realities and challenges, he had turned his back on the theoretic theology of the schools. His thinking, once done on the balcony, had moved out on to the road, had become realistic and existential. Small wonder that of all the great Christian thinkers who now engaged his interest, from Calvin to Kierkegaard, his first and greatest master was Paul, the very man whom many of his contemporaries had dismissed as the gratuitous sophisticator of the gospel, but whom he pronounced 'the fifth evangelist', declaring that an evangelist with his narrative was but an acolyte of an apostle with his *kerygma*, or gospel.

During the first three of his seven years in Cambridge Forsyth's health was very precarious; but his marriage to Bertha Ison in 1898 gave him a new hold on life. Proof of his spreading fame as a theologian came in 1899 when he was invited to cross the Atlantic and address a great Congregational Assembly in Boston on 'The Evangelical Principle of Authority', a theme to which he was to return again and again. One who heard Forsyth later wrote: 'In Forsyth's address the Council reached its climax. It was a passionate plea for the Cross as the central thing in our Christian faith. He spoke as a man inspired. He flamed, he burned . . . I wonder whether it was that great afternoon which made us realize here in England what a great gift God had given our churches in P. T. Forsyth.'[5] When Forsyth had spoken, instead of discussing what he had said, the audience rose and sang, 'In the Cross of Christ I glory'.

Two years later, in 1901, began the twenty finest years of Forsyth's life when he became Principal of what is now known as New College, London, then but recently recognized as a Divinity School by London University. Now for almost two decades, in a life crowded by college work and worries, plus the wider demands of his own denomination, Forsyth wrote no fewer than seventeen books, including most of his greatest.

In 1905 he was elected Chairman of the Congregational Union of England and Wales and delivered two memorable addresses, the first on 'A Holy Church the Moral Guide of Society', the other on 'The Grace of the Gospel as the Moral Authority in the Church'.

1907 found Forsyth in Yale for the Lyman Beecher lectures later published under the title *Positive Preaching and the Modern Mind*, and now perhaps his best-known book.

Another and less welcome share of the limelight was his involvement that year in the controversy created by R. J. Campbell's so-called 'New Theology'. This, on examination, turned out to be a Hegelian monism verging on pantheism, with a faintly Christian veneer. A. G. Gardiner ('Alpha of the Plough') ranked Campbell among the 'Prophets, Priests and Kings' of the time. Much less complimentary was Forsyth's friend, James Denney: 'It is only half-educated sophists who write "New Theologies", deceiving and being deceived.' It is but fair to add that Campbell later recanted most of his 'sophistries'.[6]

The outbreak of the First World War in 1914 brought deep distress to Forsyth who had long loved the German people and read their theology. But his own reaction to the crisis, set down in *The Christian Ethic of War* (1916), was clear and uncompromising. Germany, he held, by deliberately repudiating all moral control when it collided with her commercial interests, had forfeited every right-thinking man's respect. Force, he said, to the sorrow of the pacifists, must be met with force for conscience's sake, for the world's sake and for the kingdom's. To leave force to the non-moral world would be to leave the world to the tender mercies of the devil.

During these years of the First World War seven books came from his pen, the most powerful and prophetic being *The Justification of God* (discussed in chapter 9 below), the last being *This Life and the Next* where his ripest thought on the Christian hope of immortality is set down with wonderful simplicity and power.

When the War ended in 1918, Forsyth was over seventy and desperately tired. Ill health and disease had slowly sapped his strength, and at last on the fourth Armistice Day, 11 November 1921, he went to that God whom he had so long and nobly served.

On the memorial tablet to him in New College Chapel there stands the epitaph – and none could be apter: PER CRUCEM AD LUCEM – 'through the Cross to the Light'.

NOTES

1. *JOG*, p. 218.
2. *The Expository Times*, November 1972, p. 58.
3. *PPMM*, pp. 281f.
4. *PPJC*, p. 201.
5. J. D. Jones, *Three Score Years and Ten*, Hodder and Stoughton 1940, p. 132.
6. William R. Nicoll (ed.), *Letters of Principal James Denney to W. Robertson Nicoll*, Hodder and Stoughton 1920, p. 86.

2

Forsyth and His Writings

'His letters are weighty and strong', said some of Paul's critics, 'but his bodily presence is weak.' The same might have been said, though in no censorious sense, of Forsyth, for whom Paul was *the* apostle. In this chapter our main theme will be his writings; but we may introduce them with a word about his 'presence' and personality before we proceed to 'the style which was the man' and that 'faith-thinking' of which it was the expression.

Forsyth was neither tall nor handsome, nor was he blessed with exuberant health. But he had a fine forehead, with a large moustache and deep piercing eyes. All his life he was delicate, so that he once said that from childhood he had never known a day without pain. His was a highly-strung nature which on occasion uttered itself in sharp speech, but there was no abiding malice in it.

If his body was fragile, his mind was extraordinarily quick and, under pressure, able to work at almost demonic speed. Possessed of a gay and ready wit, he delighted in puns and *bon mots*. He had a genius for friendship and was very sympathetic to the unfortunate. But, above all, as his daughter Jessie testifies, he was 'none of your helpless, head-in-the-air professors' but (as a friend put it) 'a good man to go hunting tigers with'.

The popular image of a great theologian is of a deep-browed thinker in an ivory tower pondering the deep things of God remote from the hurly-burly of the world. To this image Forsyth firmly refuses to conform. As we have seen, in all his pastorates he threw himself heart and soul into the burning issues of the day, ecclesiastical, social, political. He had no interest in a merely academic theology or a gospel which appealed only to the West End and had 'no touch with damned souls'. In his youth and in the great cities of England he had known the problems of poverty at first hand, and he took a lively interest in the battle being joined between capitalism and socialism. The church, he held, must ever concern itself with the redemption of society; but he was alive to the danger of its aligning itself with any particular political party, as he declared that no political issue was worth action which would rend the church.

Our point here, however, is not his politics so much as the existential nature of his theology and the need for a gospel which would show not merely a private concern for individual souls but a power to redeem our egoist and materialistic society. Once, as chairman of the Congregational Union of England and Wales, he burst out, 'Do not take my arm and lead me away to the dwellings of the pound-a-weeks and the nothing-a-weeks and tell me, if I want realities, to consider there. I was there, and worked there, and considered there, and have been considering ever since.'[1] In short, for Forsyth truth – Christian truth – was always 'truth in order to goodness', truth to be lived out in the real world, truth in order to social justice and righteousness which he called 'applied holiness'. 'We are not saved,' he said, 'if we are saved into neglect of a social salvation.'

I

When we turn from the man to his writings, the first thing we note is their quantity. In some thirty years he wrote no fewer than twenty-five books (thirteen exceeding two hundred pages) plus nearly three hundred articles and contributions to other books.

The next thing we mark is the astonishing variety of the themes handled. We usually think of Forsyth as a writer on the work and person of Christ, on church and sacraments, on prayer and missions. Yet, besides books on marriage and the Christian attitude to war, he wrote volumes on art, socialism and independency as well as producing studies of the Christian aspects of evolution, Calvinism and capitalism, Hardy's pessimism and Ibsen's treatment of guilt.

The student of Forsyth should of course concentrate on his major works, which we shall mention in a moment. But if he wishes a simple introduction to Forsyth he could hardly do better than begin with *God the Holy Father*, three sermons published around the turn of the century which show the *new* Forsyth, the man who has 'found his true and magnetic North'. For the mature Forsyth he might then turn to *The Church, the Gospel and Society*, a volume which binds together his two addresses as chairman of the Congregational Union. Here he will find quintessential Forsyth, full of profound insights, characteristic judgments, and passages which linger in the memory like strains of noble music.

Having thus whetted his appetite, the student should then proceed to what are his six major works:

Positive Preaching and the Modern Mind (1907)
The Person and Place of Jesus Christ (1909)
The Work of Christ (1910)
The Principle of Authority (1913)
The Justification of God (1916)
The Church and the Sacraments (1917)

Positive Preaching is a book about preaching in the world of today, and as timely now as it was in 1907. It has little to say about what might be called 'the tricks of the trade' and much to say about the preacher's burden. Preaching is not just a man in a pulpit talking to passive hearers. It is an *act of worship* – a divine-human encounter – in which preacher and congregation share. And the burden of it is the grace of God – 'his undeserved and unbought pardon and redemption of us in face of our sin' – conceived not as a doctrine or a promise but as an act and a power of God. This act and power the preacher does not merely proclaim; he *prolongs* it. The real presence of Christ crucified and risen, as the power of God, is what makes of a speech a sermon, and what makes of a sermon a gospel. And in it all God continues his work in Christ. From this high concept of preaching, yet at the same time so loyal to the New Testament, Forsyth goes on to apply the gospel to modern man and society in a book which, as Dr F. D. Coggan has said,[2] 'is like the Word, of which it speaks so much, "living, powerful and piercing"'.

By almost universal consent *The Person and Place of Jesus Christ* (which we shall discuss fully in chapter 6 below) is his *magnum opus*. Here Forsyth's style is at its brilliant best; there are no tantalizing digressions; and Forsyth advances, step by logical step, to a solution of the mystery of the God-man which uses not metaphysical but moral categories to illumine the union of the divine and human in the eternal Son of God.

The Work of Christ ought to have been Forsyth's greatest book, for it deals with what was the master-light of all his spiritual seeing – that cross in which God honoured his own holiness at the cost of his own sacrifice and so set up his kingdom as the moral centre of history. We shall discuss it in chapter 5 below. Insights aplenty and memorable passages it contains; but it lacks system and clarity, and if we are to grasp how Forsyth conceived 'the Atoning Cross which is the Alpha and Omega of grace', we must supplement it from what he has to say elsewhere.

The Principle of Authority is Forsyth's longest, hardest and most philosophical book (we shall discuss its general theme in chapter 4 below). It deals with the perennial problem of authority, and gives us Forsyth's philosophy of religion and theory of knowledge. The question of authority in religion is studied under three heads – in relation to certainty, sanctity and society; and for his answer Forsyth goes back behind the Bible and the church to that which made them both, the gospel of God's grace – his treatment in Christ of the world's moral tragedy, God's revelation of himself breaking in on the world as redemption. Here, whatever Rome, or fundamentalist Protestantism, or Quakerism may say, is the Christian's ultimate source of authority, even if he may never hope to *prove* it to the *natural* man who, because he does not feel his need, does not recognize the authority of a Word which offers him forgiveness and reconciliation. In this book we find all Forsyth's characteristic emphases – the holiness of God, the cross as the moral centre of history, the uniqueness of the apostles' inspiration, the Bible as sacramental history, faith as self-commitment, our knowledge of God as dependent on God's prevenient knowledge of us, grace as something more than love, the primacy of the will over the intellect, the paramountcy of obedience.

The Justification of God (which we shall treat in chapter 9 below), written during the hell of the First World War, is a justification of the ways of God in a world where wickedness abounds, that is, a 'theodicy'. Philosophers and historians may attempt to find a pattern in the flux and reflux of historical events; but theodicy there is none, says Forsyth, save in a proper theology of the cross. Here we have God's key to the otherwise undecipherable riddle of history: 'the spinal chord of history is redemption'. In this book, as John Hick has said,[3] we have the eloquence and vision of a great Christian prophet; and what Forsyth has to say is as relevant today as when the book was written.

In 1917 came *The Church and the Sacraments* (to be discussed in chapter 7 below) in which Forsyth sets forth the nature of the church and his own preferred solution to the problem of 'our unhappy divisions', before going on to expound the sacraments of baptism and holy communion, which he calls 'Christ's love tokens to his Body, the Church'. Here, as in his doctrine of preaching, we have Forsyth the high churchman rather than Forsyth the Christian prophet. Repetitious and unsystematic, it none the less is replete with his characteristic insights, apophthegms, and vivid sentences. In both of the related themes of the book Forsyth thinks not only 'modernly' but 'unsectarianly'. Thus he says[4] that the affirmation 'I believe in the one Holy Catholic and Apostolic Church' sounds to him like a line of great poetry, and he declares that a mere memorialistic concept of the sacrament of the Lord's supper is a worse error than the Roman mass, as it is far less lovely.[5] All this not from an Anglo-Catholic but from the man whom Horton Davies[6] rightly pronounces 'Dissent's greatest twentieth-century theologian'.

II

We turn now to the vexed question of Forsyth's literary style. Reviewing his *Work of Christ*, James Denney wrote:[7] 'I liked Forsyth more than ever, not because he was more lucid or consecutive, but because he really strikes sparks from his anvil.' A just comment, yet not all Forsyth's readers relished the 'sparks' from Forsyth's 'anvil'. 'A shower of sky rockets,' said George Jackson. 'Fireworks in a fog,' complained Silvester Horne. Those who dislike Forsyth tend to concur. Those who like him see in him a kind of theological Carlyle who, if he can darken counsel with words, can be unforgettable when his thought runs clear and he soars into the empyrean. Here, for example, are some sentences from *The Justification of God* written in 1916 when Christians were crying out 'Why does God allow all this to happen?' 'War', Forsyth answers, 'is sin's apocalypse' and he goes on:

What is it that would justify God to you? You have grown up in an age that has not yet got over the delight of having discovered in evolution the key to creation. You saw the long series broadening to the perfect day. You saw it foreshortened in the long perspective, peak rising on peak, each successively catching the rising sun. The dark valley, antres vast, and deserts horrible you did not see. They were crumpled in the tract of time, and folded away from sight. The roaring rivers and thunders, the convulsions and voices, the awful conflicts latent in nature's ascent and man's—you could pass over these in the sweep of your glance . . . But now you have been flung into these awful valleys. You taste what it has cost, thousands of times over, to pass from range to range of those illuminated heights. You are in bloody, monstrous and deadly dark.[8]

Is it not like Carlyle describing the French Revolution? But we have not yet answered the question, Why is Forsyth's style often so difficult? It is not enough to say that he often peppers his pages with rare and *recherché* words (like 'antres' in the passage just quoted) that send you to the dictionary for their meaning. There is truth in the suggestion that he often found himself struggling in a storm of sublime thoughts, that he had too many ideas in his head all clamouring for expression. Doubtless too his love of paradox did not always make for lucidity. But this trick of style he was not slow to defend. The public, he said, likes to have the obvious flung in its face, whereupon it immediately turns the other cheek! Paradox is needed to arrest men's attention. Besides, it lies at the heart of Christianity, whether it be its dogma of the God-man, or the Christian life: 'Work out your own salvation . . . for God is at work in you' (Phil. 2.12f.).

But for the real source of Forsyth's obscurity we must delve yet deeper. Goethe wrote:

> Would you the poet understand,
> Then go you must into his land.

The reason why so many of his readers found Forsyth difficult is that they found the experience of which he wrote quite strange to themselves. He was leading them into 'land' which was unfamiliar to them. This Forsyth himself held to be the chief reason why men charged him with 'fogginess'. 'There is nothing more obscure to common sense', he said, 'than the personal experience of faith which believes in present grace, real judgment, and final good amid a world that lies in wickedness.'[9]

Yet Forsyth was not always difficult. At the end of chapter 4 below we shall quote a passage where he writes as clearly and logically as man could when discussing 'the autonomy of the Christian claim'. And not seldom he puts truth with such gnomic brevity that he has been called 'the most quotable of theologians'. Here are ten epigrams from his pen which epitomize much of his theological thought:

Half gospels have no dignity and no future. Like the famous mule, they have neither pride of ancestry nor hope of posterity.

A living heresy is better than a dead orthodoxy.

To know God is there is one thing, to know that we are known of God is another.

None but the great theologies of redemption are adequate to the great tragedies of the world.

The Cross and not the cradle holds the secret of the Lord.

An undogmatic Christ is the advertisement of a dying faith.

The peace of God is not glassy calm but mighty confidence.

The apostolic succession is the evangelical.

The seat of revelation is in the Cross, and not in the heart.

Look to the Gospel, and it will see to the experience.

To the gift of epigram he added that of apt analogy. While his friend Denney confessed that 'an illustration was his despair', it came readily to Forsyth. Every reader of *The Work of Christ* will recall how he draws out the difference between God's sacrifices and man's by the story of the Belgian signalman who, as two passenger trains were set on a collision course because the points had not been set, threw himself flat between the rails, held the tie-rod with his hands till the train had thundered over him, and then quietly arose, as in a parable from death, and returned quietly to his work. Not less apt is his illustration (to be quoted more fully later in this book) of the grandmother's gift of a christening mug to the young child, in order to teach the prevenient grace of God in the sacrament of infant baptism, when 'a Father and a Son come down in the Spirit to our little door'. Again, the idea of *kenōsis*, Forsyth holds, is necessary to any true doctrine of Christ's person. But what human analogy will serve to suggest what was involved in Christ's self-emptying? Think, answers Forsyth, of the university student with a real bent for philosophy who, on the death of his father, has to take over the family business, resigning his intellectual interests and forgetting most of what he once knew. So, in the incarnation, Christ 'consented not to know with a nescience divinely wise'.

Yet, when the final defence of Forsyth's style has to be made, lovers of his books will always point to those many passages where poet, prophet and theologian combine to give us power, beauty and truth in a manner that reminds us of Isaiah at his greatest. This, for instance, on what Pascal called the greatness and the misery of man:

We inherit greatness and breathe it. Earth and sky and day and night; stars in the naked heavens, breathings of wind, and the coming of spring; hill and plain, rolling tracts, and river and sea; the mist on the long wet moor, and above it the black, baleful cloud; fleets and camps, cities and realms; valour and power, science, trades, churches, causes, arts, charities; the fidelities of peace and the heroisms of war, the rhythm of order and the stream of progress; the generations that go under and the civilizations that survive; the energies unseen, the vanished past, the forgotten and the unforgettable brave; the majesty of the moral hero and the splendour of the public saint; agonies, love and man's unconquerable mind—Oh, we have a great world, great prospects and great allies. We inherit greatness, and we inhabit promise . . .

But as our sun rises there is a rising cloud. In the moving soul there is a frail seam, an old wound, a tender sore. The stout human heart has a wearing ache and a haunting fear. There is a hollow in the soul's centre, in its last hold no fortress, and in its sanctuary no abiding God. A vanity blights the glory of time, a lameness falls on the strenuous wing, our sinew shrinks at certain touches, and we halt on our thigh; pride falters, and the high seems low, and the hour is short, and the brief candle is out, and what is man that he is accounted of? There is a day of the Lord upon all that is haughty, on lofty tower and tall cedar, and upon all pleasant imagery. And misery, sin, and death grow great as all our triumph dwindles on the sight . . .

Yet (Forsyth goes on)

The greatness of the soul is more apparent in the greatness of its misery than in the triumph of its powers. Our spiritual failure is more than all our mighty doings. And the end—what is it? It is the Christ of God, the Saviour. We taste death, we feel decay, we face judgment. And what is the judgment of God on human guilt and woe? Lift up your eyes, lift up your hearts! Behold, the Lamb of God! It is the Saviour. Christ is God's judgment on the world. Our judgment is our salvation. His chastisement is our peace. We deserved death, and death He gave us—the death of the Cross. The end of all is the grace unspeakable, the fulness of glory—all the old splendour fixed, with never one lost good; all the spent toil garnered, all the fragments gathered up, all the lost love found for ever, all the lost purity transfigured in holiness, all the promises of the travailing soul now yea and amen, all sin turned to salvation. Eternal thanks be unto God, who hath given us the victory through Jesus Christ our Lord, and by his grace, the taste of life for every man.[10]

Here is Christian truth proclaimed with a nobility of utterance worthy of John Donne. 'Sublimity', said Longinus long ago, 'is the echo of a great soul.' Here, by any literary canons, is evidence incontrovertible that Forsyth would write in a truly grand manner. We readily forgive Shakespeare, though in many places he puzzles us and can on occasion write stark bombast. Ought we not with passages like these from Forsyth – and they are not few – to forgive him likewise, if not infrequently he darkens counsel with riddling words and perplexes us with his paradoxes?

NOTES

1. *CGS*, p. 96.
2. *The Expository Times*, August 1961, p. 324.
3. *Evil and the Love of God*, Macmillan 1966, pp. 247ff.
4. *C. and S.*, p. 42.
5. *Ibid*, p. viii.
6. *Worship and Theology in England IV: From Newman to Martineau*, Princeton University Press 1962, p. 239.
7. *Letters of Principal James Denney to W. Robertson Nicoll*, p. 239.
8. *JOG*, pp. 158f.
9. *PPJC*, pp. 297f.
10. *GHF*, pp. 78f.

3

Forsyth as Biblical Scholar

One of the supreme strengths of Forsyth's theology is that it is
biblically based as few modern theologies are. On the Bible he
bottoms all his theological thinking – not on modern science,
psychology or philosophy. It is not that he is unaware of what
the scientists or the sages or the literary luminaries of the day
are saying. He knows the theory of evolution as Huxley has
expounded it, and while not denying its truth in the realm of
biology, finds that it gives no sure clue to the meaning of history
or warrants any kind of belief in a law of inevitable and
irresistible progress to paradise on earth. He has read Tolstoy
and Bernard Shaw, and can even find in sceptics like Thomas
Hardy and agnostics like Ibsen unwitting 'tutors unto Christ'.
But for Forsyth, as for the dying Sir Walter Scott, 'there is but
one Book', a book about God in a sense in which no other book
is, and which therefore ought to be the preacher's inexhaust-
ible fountain of divine truth. 'If you would preach a classical
gospel,' he says, 'give your nights and days, your head and
heart, to converse with the Bible.'[1]

But Forsyth is no ordinary Bible scholar. He is one of
uncommon penetration and (as we shall see) prescience. It is
sometimes said that the professors who teach systematic
theology (as Forsyth did) are twenty or thirty years behind the
biblical scholars. Forsyth was in fact twenty or thirty years
ahead of most of them. He needed none to tell him what the
most advanced German critics were saying, as he could put his
finger on their weaknesses as well as their strengths. But the
gospel was not at the mercy (as the faint hearts supposed) of

'the science of Tübingen' or anywhere else, because the Bible was not a document but a sacramental book. Both it and the church were made by something *in* them, but *before* and *above* them – the historic grace of God, revealed first to old Israel and consummated in Christ and his cross. For the gospel was an experienced fact, a living Word, before it was a written one.

To begin with, then, let us consider Forsyth's general approach to the Bible.

I

The man who spoke of 'the Holy Spirit's gift of critical scholarship' was clearly no fundamentalist. 'To stake the Gospel on the absolute inerrancy of the Bible', he said,[2] 'is to commit, in a Protestant way, the Roman error of staking the sacrament on the correctitude of its ritual or the ordination of the priest.' Modern scholarship had in fact made the Bible a new book. Consider (he said) how the critics (e.g. George Adam Smith) had restored the prophets to the church. Criticism had a valuable function to perform – even if it was only 'the hand-maid of the Gospel – downstairs'. It helped us to 'disengage the kernel from the husk, to save the time so often lost in the defence of outposts, and to discard obsolete weapons and superfluous baggage'.[3] By so doing, it cleared the ground for the erection of a house of doctrine in which the component materials could be chosen according to their real strength.

But if Forsyth was no hard-shell fundamentalist, hurling the Bible whole and harsh at the heads of those who read it other-wise, he could go so far as to say:[4] 'The true minister ought to find the Bible so full of spiritual food and felicity that he has some difficulty in not believing in verbal inspiration.'

But, next – and here we see how far ahead of his times he was – at a time when the analytical criticism of the Bible was at its height, with German savants splitting documents as minutely as the old scholastics used to split dialectical hairs – in short, 'taking the Bible apart,' as the coloured man com-plained of his minister's dissection of the Bible, 'and unable to put it together again' – Forsyth had already passed from analysis, with all its pains and gains (e.g. the source criticism of the gospels) to *synthesis*, 'putting the Bible together again' with the help of an enlightened criticism, as C. H. Dodd has done for so many in our time. Listen to what Forsyth wrote in 1905:

The critical treatment of the Bible must have its place. Let us not make fools of ourselves by denying it. We shall be fighting against God and resisting the Spirit...But its place is secondary, ancillary. It has little place in a pulpit . . . The critical study of the scripture is at its best, and the higher criticism at its highest when it passes from being merely analytic and becomes synthetic. And the synthetic principle in the Bible is the gospel.[5]

In all the varieties of biblical religion Forsyth discerned its fundamental unity. What we have in the Bible is sacramental history, history with a drift – the drift of God's ongoing purpose of grace, prefigured in the Old Testament, and consummated in the New. He said,

The Gospel of grace in Christ, the purpose and at last the act of redemption is the key to the Bible. It makes the Bible not a mere chronicle, nor a mere set of annals, but history of the greatest kind . . . In Christ we have the culmination of the long revealing line of Old Testament prophecy. We have in a whole permanent personality what the prophets had in their fleeting vision. We have God seeking and finding and saving us. God tells us through man's word, or by his own deeds, the secret of his purpose. To carry home this is the object of the Bible. For this the Bible exists. From this the Bible sprang.[6]

Accordingly, the Bible unity is a dramatic unity of action issuing in a great historical crescendo, the coming of the reign of God in Christ's ministry, death, resurrection and in the advent of the Spirit. As proof that Christ himself so read the scriptures we need look no further than his parable of The Wicked Tenants (Mark 12.1–9).

It is worth while to dwell a moment on this point. In these days when we study the Bible critically, some people are upset when they find Jesus assuming that King David wrote Ps. 110, and would evidently fault him for not knowing all the answers

33

to problems of authorship which even our pundits today cannot solve. But where Jesus was infallible was not in literary criticism but in his grasp of his Father and his Father's purpose for him. Only the very naive would expect him to play the role of first-century literary critic and trace, let us say, three different hands in the prophecies of Isaiah. Not so did Christ treat the scriptures, nor should we expect him to do so:

> Christ used the Bible as a means of grace, not as a manual of Hebrew or other history . . . He found in it the long purpose and deep scope of God's salvation . . . He cared little for what our scholars expound—the religion of Israel . . . What he found (in the Old Testament) was not the prophets' thoughts of God but God's invasion of them and their race by words and deeds of gracious power . . . The torch he carried through the Old Testament was the Gospel of grace . . . He read it with the eyes of faith, not of science . . . And he read it as a whole.[7]

This is finely and truly said. But Forsyth went further. The great test of a religion is religious. Christianity will not stand or fall by its critical attitude to the document, but by its faithful attitude to the gospel. We do not need further histories of Israel. What we need is a well equipped modern scholar, in the mould of Jonathan Edwards, to give us a history of redemption, both in the Old Testament and the New.[8] Perhaps we are still waiting for that book. But years after Forsyth men like A. G. Hebert (in his *The Throne of David*) and those who essayed, however unsuccessfully, to write Christian theologies of the Old Testament, had a clear inkling of what Forsyth was after – a history of redemption.

Redemption, be it noted, not merely revelation. For him, revelation was not the communication of a series of divinely-inspired truths; nor, again, did he regard revelation as God, so to speak, drawing back the veil that divides the seen from the unseen world in order to show himself, in a theophany, to earth-born mortals. As we shall see in the next chapter, revelation was ever, for Forsyth, redemptive. In Christ God did not merely show himself but came and acted, redeemingly

34

and decisively. Or, to put the matter in one of Forsyth's favourite phrases, 'In Christ God was his own apostle'.

II

As we turn now to the New Testament, let us remember that Forsyth was writing roughly between the end of the Boer War and the conclusion of the First World War. To remember this is to realize how 'modern' (in the best sense of the word) he is in so many of his insights into the meaning of the New Testament. So much of what is now the common currency of New Testament science and theology you will find in books and articles he wrote sixty years ago.

Let us take three examples, one touching the nature of religion, the second the character of the gospels, and the third the doctrine of apostolic inspiration.

Some of us remember the impact Rudolf Otto made on the theological world just after the First World War by his book on *The Idea of the Holy*. The essence of religion, he said, lay not in knowledge or in conduct but in awe – in the sense of the utter holiness of God. But long before Otto Forsyth had been declaring[9] that 'the holiness of God is the real foundation of religion', reminding his readers that the first petition of the Lord's Prayer is 'Hallowed be thy name', and correcting wrong notions of the love of God: 'Love is not evangelical till it has dealt with holy law. In the midst of the rainbow there is a throne.'[10]

The early 1920s saw the rise in Germany of the Form Critics, like Bultmann and Dibelius. The gospels, they said, are not biographies; they are religious documents written 'from faith to faith'. But this was something Forsyth had long been saying. 'Pamphlets in the service of the Church' was his description of them,[11] written for people who had already received the gospel, or had the epistles, to fill out their knowledge of Christ. Moreover, 'they are engrossed with Christ not as a fascinating character but as the gospel to us of the active grace of God.'

In 1918 Barth startled the theological world by his exegesis of the Epistle to the Romans in which he took a new and high view of apostolic inspiration. The letters of the apostles were true vehicles of revelation because their subject matter was the Spirit of Christ, and in them that Spirit spoke his saving truth through chosen and commissioned witnesses. But in 1905 Forsyth had written:[12] 'Christ represents grace as incarnate, they (the apostles) as inspired.' In them he unfolds his finished work. The epistles give the key to the gospels, as the prophets do to Old Testament history . . . 'In the gospels Christ appears as acting, in the Epistles Christ interprets his own action.'

These and other trends were to bring a new depth to New Testament studies. In Britain it came in the late 1920s, especially in the work of Sir Edwyn Hoskyns. But most of what Hoskyns, Dodd and others were to teach us in the 1930s had already been anticipated, a quarter of a century before by Forsyth.

III

To illustrate this new depth in understanding of the New Testament, let us take the kingdom of God, the person and work of Christ, and the apostolic gospel, or *kērygma*.

Nowadays scholars are agreed that the dominant theme of the Synoptic Gospels is the kingdom, or reign, of God and that it is to be interpreted dynamically and eschatologically. But in the first decade of the century men were still explaining the kingdom of God as some kind of Christian commonwealth to be built upon the principle of Jesus, or construing it as a christianized version of evolution. 'First the blade, then the ear, then the full corn in the ear – what is that,' said Henry Drummond, 'but evolution?'

Now, thanks to Schweitzer, Otto, Dodd and the rest, we know that the kingdom of God in the gospels, so far from being a human creation, is a divine invasion. It means God breaking into history in his royal power to visit and redeem his people from their sins, and the new order of things thus established: all, in fact, that nowadays we sum up in the phrase 'inaugurated eschatology'.

But, years before, Forsyth, if he had not cleared up all the problems, had got to the heart of the matter. 'The kingdom of God', he wrote,[13] 'is the emergence into the life of history, both by growth and crisis, of that saving Sovereignty which is the moral power and order of the spiritual world.' And he was just as sure as our modern exegetes that in the gospels the reign of God is not just a shining hope on the far horizon but an inbreaking reality in the work of Jesus. 'The Cross', he declared,[14] 'is not the preliminary of the Kingdom; it is the Kingdom breaking in.'

Towards the end of his life Karl Barth told us that he began by thinking that Jesus was the prophet of the kingdom and later came to see that he *was* the kingdom. But in 1909 Forsyth had reached this conclusion. He wrote:

Like Messiah, the Kingdom was an Old Testament phrase which served to enclose what he brought in himself; and the picture, the phrase, was broken when the light shone. The Kingdom was great with him. The Gospel of the Kingdom was Christ in essence; Christ was the Gospel of the Kingdom in power. The Kingdom was Christ in a mystery; Christ was the publication, the establishment of the Kingdom . . . He was the truth of his own greatest Gospel. It is wherever he is. To have him is to ensure it.[15]

Of a piece with all this is his reading of the story of Jesus, in whose mission and message the kingdom invaded history. In Forsyth's time men were still trying to squeeze Jesus into the moulds of human psychology or to place him in the succession of spiritual genius. In the result they produced a lay figure quite incapable of accounting for the rest of the New Testament. The liberals (and they have their successors today) tried to tell the story of Jesus without a theology. Like Schweitzer, Forsyth said it could not be done. Only a Christ whose leading motives were theological, whose destiny was forefated for him by his Father's will and purpose, could make sense of the gospel story or the thing he was to accomplish for God at Jerusalem when he embraced the cross. Jesus, said Forsyth, broke his nation on a theology. He knew that his death would 'throw his people in the wrong'. This was the essence of his agony. Loving his people, he yet knew that he must be their doom. And so 'amid the judgment' he offered his obedience to God for his kingdom and made the sacrifice required by obedience to his Father's will. Listen to Forsyth describing Christ's grief over Jerusalem because 'it did not recognize God's moment when it came' (Luke 19.44):

It was the agony of an old nation not only dying but damned; and all its vast tragedy transpiring not only within the soul of one Man but (chief horror!) by the solemn choice and awful act of that one Man himself, and he its lover. Think of a whole nation proud, passionate and stubborn, with an ingrained belief in a world prerogative and mission, expiring in one Man, in whom also by a dreadful collision was rising the Kingdom of God they had forsworn; and the fate of God's whole Kingdom in the world decided in an Armageddon of that one spirit; a world's eternal warfare and destiny forced through the channel of one soul vast enough, whatever he did not know or could not know, to be in his death alive and adequate to such an issue.[16]

This beyond all question represents the mind of Jesus as he faced the cross.

Now consider what Forsyth had to say about the gospel which the apostles preached. In spite of I Cor. 15.1–11, it had become almost an axiom with the liberals that, *vis-à-vis* the other apostles, Paul in his version of the gospel was in a minority of one. Not till 1936 was this delusion finally exploded by C. H. Dodd's *Apostolic Preaching* which showed that 'in the beginning was the *kērygma*', that long before any written gospels appeared – before even Paul began to write – there was a common apostolic gospel – a *kērygma* preached by all the apostles. But as early as 1905 Forsyth was pointing out that not only do the epistles antedate the gospels (thus disproving the suggestion that their theology is a later development) but that they reflect 'the common faith of the apostolic community' and not just the idiosyncrasies of Paul; and in 1913 he wrote: 'In the matter of the vital creative meaning of Christ's person and death, Peter, Paul and John were all of one mind ... There was of course no universal theological formula, there was not an orthodoxy; but certainly there was a common apostolic Gospel, a *kērygma*. And this theological *kērygma* stands for us as the common chord in the three great names who represent the apostolate.[17]

But Forsyth was not merely content to assert that on their basic gospel the apostles all agreed. He went on to claim that in the apostles Christ unfolded the meaning of the work which God had sent him into the world to do. In the apostolic writings we find Christ continuing to teach, and lead, and save. We have a finished redemption energizing in the apostles as revelation: 'The apostolic documents are the prolongation of the message of Jesus. They are Christ himself interpreting his finished work through men in whom not they lived but he lived in them. Christ in his apostles interpreted his finished work as truly as in his life-time he interpreted his unfinished work.'[18]

IV

All this may serve to introduce what Forsyth has to say about the man Forsyth called 'the fifth evangelist'. 'Christ taught Paul in the Spirit,' he wrote, 'as truly as he taught the disciples in the flesh.' When Paul said 'We have the mind of Christ' (I Cor. 2.16), he meant 'we have the theology of Christ'. A man who writes thus obviously found Paul's exposition of the common apostolic gospel *sympathisch* and had an intuitive insight into its emphases and meanings. As the apostle gloried in the cross (Gal. 6.14), so did Forsyth. For him it was the centre of history and of the moral universe, the key to Christian ethics and the clue to God's final dealings with the world. In the next chapter we shall have to expound Forsyth's doctrine of the atonement. It will therefore suffice here to quote J. K. Mozley who was the first Anglican to appraise Forsyth at his true spiritual stature: 'Forsyth goes round and round like a thunderstorm, but again and again he returns back on his tracks as though he could not bear to be out of sight of the lights of home, the home that Christ made for men by his Cross, the home which in a very real sense for Forsyth was the Cross.'[19]

For Paul, faith was sinful man's life-response to the grace

of God in the cross of Christ. 'The life that I now live in the flesh,' he said, 'I live by faith in the Son of God who loved me and gave himself for me' (Gal. 2.20). And we recall how in Rom. 4 Paul singles out Abraham as a supreme exemplar of it – the man who, when God spoke to him, took God at his word – and obeyed. Just so Forsyth declared, 'Faith is taking God at his word – at his living Word, Christ';[20] and once he defined Christian faith memorably as 'the grand venture in which we commit our whole soul and future to the confidence that Christ is not an illusion but the reality of God'.[21] Likewise, as Paul spoke of 'faith working through love' (Gal. 5.6), Forsyth called love 'the rose-bloom of Christian faith', and declared,[22] 'The good live by faith and work by love. Never did Paul dream that his song of Christian love would be turned to belittle or belabour the Christian faith on which alone it grows!'

Pauline students agree that 'in Christ' is a key-phrase in his letters. But what does it mean? For decades it was taken to describe the individual believer's mystical fellowship with his living Lord. But is this the whole truth? Does it not carry strong corporate overtones? Nowadays all scholars agree that it does. (Note how the New English Bible in such passages as Eph. 1.1; Phil. 1.1 and Col. 1.2 is concerned to bring this out with its 'incorporate in Christ'.) But, long before, Forsyth had seen that to be 'in Christ' is to be a member of Christ's society, the church. 'To be a Christian,' he wrote, 'is not to attach one's salvation to a grand individual, but it is to enter Christ, and to enter Christ is in the same act to enter the Church which is in Christ. Faith in Christ is faith in One whose indwelling makes a Church, and who carries a Church within his corporate person.'[23]

Mention of the 'corporate Christ' suggests another instance of Forsyth's fidelity to the New Testament. When its writers speak of the work of Christ, they do so in a *racial* way. Salvation is far more than the nexus of the individual, *qua* individual, with the Saviour. As Christ had declared that he was giving his life to ransom 'all men' (for *polloi* in Mark 10.45, as in Rom. 5.15, is a Hebrew way of saying 'all') so Paul and

John declare that Christ died for the sins of the whole race. Protestantism, however, had come to think of the cross as 'a life-saving apparatus for personal escape' and tended to preach 'an individualist salvation by private bargain'. This, for Forsyth, was a travesty of the historic gospel: 'It took a world's salvation to save me,' and he went on: 'Christ was in his victory the agent of the race . . . He was no mere lone individual . . . If he overcame the world, it was humanity that won. If Christ died for all, all died in the Act. We rise because he rose; and we rise not like him but in him,'[24] To all this the apostle would have said Amen.

V

This chapter may fitly end with two more examples which show how penetrating was Forsyth's insight into the New Testament.

During the last forty years scholars have been re-discovering the true meaning of the *ecclēsia*, or church, as the people of God. In the Septuagint *ecclēsia* normally translates the Hebrew *qahal*, the usual Old Testament word for the gathered people of God. Thus when the early Christians styled themselves the *ecclēsia tou theou*, they were claiming to be the true people of God which had served itself heir to the promises made to old Israel who, by rejecting their Messiah, had rejected their vocation and destiny in him. If, then, in the New Testament we read of local congregations called *ecclēsiai* (plural), these are not discrete churches but outcrops of the one great church. 'The local church', says K. L. Schmidt in his magisterial article on the subject in the Gerhard Kittel's *Theological Dictionary of the New Testament*, 'was conscious of itself as being the representative of the universal Church'.

Long before Schmidt Forsyth had seized the point and made it much more vividly. 'What the apostles planted,' he said, 'was not churches but stations of the Church. What the Gospel created was not a crowd of churches but one church in various places. What we have everywhere is the one Church of Christ put down here and there, looking out in Corinth, Ephesus, or Thessalonica.'[25]

Or consider the true nature of preaching. How does the preacher differ from the orator, the politician or the propagandist? Consult great modern heralds of the gospel like H. H. Farmer and J. S. Stewart, and you find them agreed that preaching is a part of God's saving activity. In the act of preaching God's salvation in Christ continues, the gospel reverberates. Then we turn up Forsyth's *Positive Preaching and the Modern Mind* written in 1907, to find this: 'Preaching is the Gospel prolonging and declaring itself. The gift of God's grace was, and is, his work of Gospel. And it is this Act which is prolonged in the word of the preacher and not merely declared.'[26]

A new concept of preaching? No, as old as the apostle who called the gospel 'the power of God unto salvation' (Rom. 1.16) and claimed that in the word of his 'ambassador', Christ himself speaks his saving word (II Cor. 5.18–20). Properly understood Christian preaching is the dynamic medium through which God contemporizes his historic and redemptive self-revelation in Christ and his cross, and offers men the chance of responding to it by the obedience of faith.

Our discussion has shown that in his task as a systematic theologian (though he could be exasperatingly unsystematic himself) Forsyth brought to matters biblical, and especially the New Testament, an insight unmatched by any of his contemporary *Systematikers*. One of them, James Denney, claimed in a letter to W. Robertson Nicoll that Forsyth had 'more true and important things to say than any other man writing theology' and in another, that Forsyth's shining merit was that he always kept returning to the New Testament and the apostolic gospel.[27] We suggest that the second letter contains the secret and clue to the claim made in the first.

Since Forsyth's day the revival in biblical theology has come and – some would say – gone. We seem to be moving back again to an anthropocentric version of Christianity instead of the God-centred one which Forsyth expounded with such passion and power. New 'gospels' are being peddled which seek to accommodate Christianity to the spirit of the age. Its protagonists 'demythologize' the New Testament, or rather seek to expound its 'myths' in the existential philosophy of Heidegger and others, invite us to glorify man in the depths of his being and to see in Jesus 'the Man for others'. Had he been alive today Forsyth would have agreed with Barth that this is 'flat-tyre theology' because all the *pneuma* (which is Greek for both 'air' and 'spirit') has gone out of it. Promising to give us Christianity without tears, they all too often give us tears without Christianity, and its expounders become preachers without a real message. *Vis-à-vis* these modern hierophants, we may fairly claim that Forsyth is 'the prophet for today' because he diagnoses the needs of the human heart at a deeper level and has a far profounder grasp of the historic New Testament gospel and its adequacy to minister to our abiding human predicament.

To sum up. To Forsyth, grateful for all the new light thrown on the Bible by the critics, the Bible was, above all else, 'the sacramental book', not only the record of God's redeeming revelation in Christ but to the man of faith, prepared to hear what it has to say, a continuing means of grace. We have, said Forsyth, but one great sacrament – that of God's grace to sinful men in the cross of Christ. In this sacrament the Bible takes the place of the elements in holy communion, as it can mediate God's grace no less than they. When therefore does the Bible become authoritative for you and me? The answer is: when, through the Holy Spirit's light and leading, it mediates to us the historic grace of God. Then the old words become luminous with the passage through them of the Holy Spirit, the wire glows with the current, and the soul of the Bible stills and settles us with the grace of God. When this happens, the Bible has done its work, not as a historic document but as a historic means of grace, as a servant of the eternal gospel.

NOTES

1. *TGAA*, p. 41.
2. *Ibid*, p. 46.
3. *PPMM*, p. 280.
4. *Ibid*, p. 38.
5. *TGAA*, p. 24.
6. *Ibid*, pp. 20ff.
7. *Ibid*, pp. 34f.
8. *Ibid*, p. 52.
9. *COC*, p. 22.
10. *GHF*, p. 5.
11. *TGAA*, p. 27.
12. *Ibid*, pp. 30f.
13. *TLTN*, p. 60.
14. *JOG*, p. 77.
15. *PPJC*, p. 123.
16. *The Expositor*, July 1915.
17. *POA*, pp. 126f.
18. *PPJC*, p. 60.
19. *C. and S.*, p. viii.
20. *GHF*, p. 18.
21. *PPJC*, p. 201.
22. *C. and S.*, p. 22.
23. *Ibid*, p. 40.
24. *JOG*, p. 220.
25. *C. and S.*, p. 68.
26. *PPMM*, pp. 5f.
27. *Letters of Principal James Denney to W. Robertson Nicoll*, pp. 100, 118.

PART TWO

4

Revelation as Redemption

The Christian church claims to be the recipient and trustee of a special self-revelation of God in history. How did Forsyth construe this word 'revelation'? How did he describe the knowledge of God that we get through faith when we accept that revelation? How did he uphold the autonomy of the Christian claim? These are the questions to be answered in this chapter.

But, first, it will be helpful to set down four axioms of Forsyth's thinking.

First, true religion puts us *en rapport* with the reality of the world rather than *au fait* with its rationality.

Second, the highest reality is that of persons in inter-personal relations. Thus we are concerned with life and action – with morality. The truth we see depends on the men we are; and when the truth confronts us, it calls for our commitment. The ultimate reality is a supreme will. With it our will is our contact. Faith is therefore basically obedience.

Third, true religion feeds on concrete facts and events. Without them, religion easily degenerates into rationalism or mysticism. Therefore the media of a true knowledge of God are historical experiences.

Fourth, there is no access for the soul to the last reality of the universe, no 'Rock of Ages' for the race, except through sinful man's experience of God's forgiving grace in the cross. Here the Holy God coped with moral evil for good and all. Our footing, therefore, whether in history or morals, is the cross.

Once again we see how biblical is Forsyth's thinking. And

to his thinking about God, Christ and men Forsyth brings 'the experiential motif of a Wesley, the theological vigour and earthiness of a Luther, the moral passion of a Maurice, and the world-embracing kingdom concept of a Ritschl'.[1]

I

Nowadays we use the word 'revelation' to describe all sorts of disclosures and events. But 'revelation' is in origin a religious word and denotes divine self-disclosure. What is the proper Christian view of it? It is a question Forsyth often discusses,[2] and his answer is always the same. Revelation comes not in a *statement*, or in a *picture*, but in a *person* and his consummatory act – Christ and the cross – and it brings with it not merely new light but new life. Revelation is really redemption, and it is a thing of the heart and the soul and the will and the mind.

Why does Forsyth insist that revelation is really that old-fashioned thing redemption, a word that suggests old folios, dead divines, an outmoded evangelicalism, and revivalist hymns of yester-year? Surely, in these modern days, we ought to think of revelation as something bigger and less *borné*? Is there no divine revelation in the created world around us, in the starry heavens which declare the glory of God, in the perfection of the human form –

> If Mary is so beautiful,
> What must her Maker be? –

in the heroic self-sacrifice of a Captain Oates or a Maximilian Kolbe, the saint of Ausschwitz?

To deny that God reveals himself in such things and people, says Forsyth, would be foolish. But such revelation is so general as to be ineffectual. It only suggests God; it does not assure us of him. And it suggests God to individuals rather than to the world. What we sinners need for our cure is revelation given in history, in a person and on a racial scale, which brings us not simply light but 'newness of life'.

The 'statement' view of revelation is that dear to hard-shell

46

'fundamentalists'. What we have in the bible is a compendium of divine truths, supernaturally and infallibly written down. But the Bible is not an arsenal of Christian evidences, neither does God save the world by authorship. What we have in it is not an inerrant but a sacramental book, a book that can, by the Holy Spirit's help, mediate to the believer the historic grace of God.

Neither is the 'picture' view of revelation satisfactory, though it is an improvement on the 'statement' one. This conceives of God, in a 'theophany', so to speak drawing aside the curtain that separates the seen from the unseen world and displaying himself for men to see. On this view, the cross for instance, becomes a picture which reveals in one crowning moment of history what God is like for ever, just as from a volcano there may flash forth a spurt of flame, showing in a moment, the elemental fire that burns for ever at earth's core.

But, says Forsyth, for his saving sinful man requires more than a picture or a theophany. We are sinners, not sages. What we need is not merely illumination but redemption. The only kind of redemption which matches our need is one in which God not only comes in history but acts in it, decisively, for our salvation. Revelation must therefore be redemptive. And thus does the New Testament construe the word. 'In Christ,' says Forsyth, 'God was his own apostle.' In Christ he gave us not merely his portrait but his presence. 'In Christ God was reconciling the world to himself', giving himself in action. God came in his Son and above all in his Son's cross. Christ was God enacting his holy love to us sinners, meeting our sin with his grace. And there is no other way for God to reveal himself to sinful men than by dying for them.[3]

To understand revelation as redemption, think of a tuning-fork, says Forsyth. 'God smote on the world in Christ's act of redemption; it sounded in the apostles' word of reconciliation; and it reverberated, and goes on doing so, in the Bible.'[4]

There are thus three constituent factors in revelation: (1) God's historic act in Christ; (2) the apostles' inspired interpretation of that act in their preaching; and (3) the Bible and the church's preaching in which the gospel of God's grace in Christ prolongs itself, by the Holy Spirit's power.

Thus 'the Word of God' is not a book but God revealing himself by word and deed to man. This revelation is consummated in Christ and his atoning cross. Christ is God's unique and living Word, in whom he reconciles the world to himself. But the apostles' proclamation is also the word of God because through it the living Christ interprets his finished work to men. This word, or gospel, prolongs itself today whenever and wherever the apostolic message is faithfully preached. Thus (to sum up) as it comes from God, the Word is Christ his Son; as it comes from Christ, through his church, it is the apostolic gospel interpreted by the Holy Spirit; and the Bible itself becomes the word of God when, by the Spirit's power, the historic grace of God in Christ is mediated to believing men.

II

We have been talking about God's redeeming self-disclosure to men in Christ and the cross. It is but the other side of the same coin if now we ask, How does Forsyth conceive and interpret our knowledge of God?

We have seen that while not denying a general revelation, Forsyth's interest lay in that special revelation which God made to Israel and consummated in Christ.

Accordingly he defined Christianity as 'nothing less than habitual communion with a God of holy love on the basis of a historic revelation and redemption'.[5] This God-initiated personal communion in Christ is one in which, if it is to be real, man must knowingly share. And the knowledge which the Christian thus gains of God is of a holy Father who, having spoken by the prophets, came to save in his Son, and who now conveys himself through the Holy Spirit.

Here we note two things. First, we have in essence Forsyth's doctrine of the Trinity. For, as he put it, 'the old theologians were right when they insisted that the work of redemption was the work of the whole Trinity – Father, Son and Spirit; as we express it when we baptize into the new life of reconcilement in the three-fold name'.[6] Second, our knowledge of God is not a matter of inference – does not come by laborious excogitation or swift intuiting – but through personal encounter with the transcendent God in the person of Christ. In him, as in no one else, God is 'the Urgent Presence', making his demand on us and calling for our decision.

Thus our knowledge of God has three characteristics. First, 'our knowledge of God is the result of his revelation. We find him because he first finds us'.[7] The unique thing in religion is not a God whom we know but a God who knows us. Religion turns not on knowing but on being known. This is not absolute knowledge, says Forsyth, but the knowledge that we are absolutely known in the sense of being destined, sought and searched, like the man in Ps. 139.

Accordingly, second, our knowledge of God is not scientific or theoretic but personal, moral, existential. It belongs to that order of knowledge where person meets person – 'real life is meeting' – where the percipient person meets person and not a person a thing, as a potter a pot. Above all, it is the encounter of unholy man with holy God – the experience (to borrow Buber's language) of an Eternal Thou's infinite and creative knowledge of us which first creates our trust in him.

And what of faith's answer to the Eternal Thou? Again, it is not theoretic but personal, the response of a will to a Will, the personal power to know as we are divinely known. As the response of a whole finite person to a whole Person, absolute and holy, it is by its very nature ethical, and not merely sympathetic or impressive.

Third: the place in history where, above all, we are known by the great Knower is the cross: 'In Christ there is a spot where we are known far more than we know. There is a place where God not only speaks but comes, and not only vouches but gives, and gives not only himself to the soul, but, by a vast crisis, the soul to itself and the world to his Son.'[8]

There, at the cross, the grace of God which magnifies our guilt, in the act of mastering it, takes away our doubt, and trust gives us the security denied to sight. All this means that God's redemptive revelation of himself in Christ and his cross shapes and decides our knowledge of God. There at the cross God deals with our sin as One who eternally and lovingly knows us.

What then do we gain when, by the obedience of faith, we respond to God's redeeming revelation in Christ? In the faith that answers revelation God does not prove himself to us. He *comes home*. We gain the glad and gracious knowledge that we are forgiven. In the forgiving, loving knowledge of God we find our rest and peace. We have the certainty of a God able to bring man's will and conscience into harmony with a universe whose last reality is moral.

The question of the source of our knowledge of God leads on to that of religious authority. Where and how are we to find something outside ourselves and our opinions which will impose itself on us with power not only in family and civic life but in religion – this is the problem, old and ever new.

In his day Forsyth found Protestantism drifting about 'in an uncharted sea of liberty' like a rudderless ship, and lacking any real sense of a final and commanding spiritual authority. Where was this source of authority to be found? Answer this question, he said, and you will solve society's problems as well as the church's, for society can only be saved by that which saves the soul.

As a matter of Christian history three very different solutions have been proposed. Roman Catholicism solves the problem in terms of an authoritative church and a pope who, when he speaks *ex cathedra*, is infallible. In the result all too often faith becomes faith in an institution and grace a 'substance' which the church dispenses. Traditional Protestantism solves it in terms of an inerrant book – the word 'incartulate' and infallible. In modern times Protestants have generally sought to derive authority from individual religious experiences – the testimony of the soul.

None of these three answers satisfied Forsyth. Rome's answer might be defended if the church were really an extension of the incarnation. But how can the church which is sinful be the continuation of the life of One who knew no sin? As for the letter of her creeds, they can no more be final than the letter of scripture. As for traditional Protestantism's answer modern biblical criticism has stultified it – except for hard-shell fundamentalists. Nor can Forsyth base religious authority entirely on so subjective a thing as individual religious experience. To be sure, the new stress on experience is a salutary reaction from the formalism and literalism that had settled like a blight on the church. Yet such experience is always distorted by sin, tends to be impressive rather than regenerative, and is apt to sit loose to the historical Christ and decline into mystical slush.

So, for his answer Forsyth goes back behind both church and Bible to that which created both – the gospel of God's grace. 'Christ', he said, 'did not come to bring a Bible but a Gospel. The Bible arose afterwards from the gospel to serve the Gospel. The Bible, the preacher and the Church are made by the same thing, the Gospel.'[9] And by the 'gospel' Forsyth meant God's cure in Christ for the world's moral wreck, as it finds classical expression in John 3.16 and Rom. 5.8.

This had been essentially Luther's solution. At the Reformation he went back to 'the Bible within the Bible.' For the Reformation was the discovery of this very thing. It stood not so much for the supremacy of the individual conscience as for the rescue of the conscience by Christ's supremacy in it – Christ conceived not as a supreme rabbi who solved cases but Christ as the author and principle of a new life which solves cases by an indwelling grace and power.

Here we have still our master-clue to the riddle of authority. If Protestantism has any meaning, said Forsyth, the *ground* of our faith is identical with the *object* of it – which is God in Christ reconciling the world to himself.

Accordingly, if our need is to be met, our religious authority must be moral, social, historical, personal, living and present. Where can we find one to satisfy all these conditions? There can be but one answer: 'the grace of God to the conscience in the historic and perennial cross of Christ'.[10] Here we have not only the final seat of authority but the one true source of morals. For all morals are merely academic which do not grapple seriously with the most formidable fact in social ethics – human sin and guilt. He who can master this fact is master of the conscience, and therefore of human life, society and history. The source of authority for all mankind, in their affairs and in their faith, is our redeemer from moral death. It is the Christ who himself has satisfied the holy law which we can break but never unseat and who still reigns from his cross, through the power of the Holy Spirit. Only he can restore to us the life we have thrown away and lost the power to regain. Therefore, for Forsyth, the ultimate source of authority lies in 'the living Word and Gospel of Jesus Christ the crucified, living and royal Redeemer, present now as ever to meet the need both of our soul and of our society'.[11]

Church, Bible, religious experience – what are they but channels of this authority – the historic gospel of God's grace to our conscience in Christ, mediated now by the Spirit and authenticated in his own experience to every man who commits his life to the gracious God who meets him with forgiveness in Christ and his cross. This gospel is authoritative because of its power to disburden man of his sin and guilt and create him anew.

And what is this but a moral miracle, for there is no miracle like that which can change the whole direction and complexion of a will? In this gospel of grace alone we have that which will plant our feet on the rock of spiritual reality.

IV

If we have been interpreting Forsyth aright, he is claiming that the Christian has a special knowledge of God based on the redemptive revelation of God's grace in the historic and perennial Christ, in which he finds a final authority for the church's life and for his own. How bold a claim it is! It is the claim that the gospel carries within itself its own criterion or guiding principle, and need not await the *Nihil Obstat* of scientist, philosopher or historian. But is the claim not warranted? What panel of scientific experts, for example, can decide the truth or falsity of the gospel's central claim that 'in Christ God was reconciling the world to himself'? In other words, the supernatural truth of the gospel can only be proved by supernatural, or super-rational, experience.

None the less, the objector may well demur that Forsyth's is a high-handed way of settling the whole issue in advance by dogma. Not so, replies Forsyth, for you cannot prove the divinity of Christ except to those who have been saved by him. It is not a matter of dogma but of experience.

But the issue – the autonomy of the Christian claim – is so important that we must hear Forsyth in his own words joining issue with the objector. It is as dexterous a piece of dialectic as you will find anywhere in his writings.[12] He begins by carrying the war into his opponents' camp: 'You are settling the matter in advance by dogma,' says the critic. Retorts Forsyth,

How then do you propose to settle it? You tell me that you proceed by the canons of reason. You will go by those methods which a long and sifted experience has shown to be fruitful in the religion of research, historical and philosophical. You pursue your inquiry then on such positive principles. These canons are settled for you before you embark on your research.

Well, what objection do you have to describing these as dogmas given you in advance of your inquiry, and made obligatory in the church of science? Who would listen to science from a man who abjured the inductive methods of observation and experiment, who discarded these dogmas? You reply that these principles, these formulas, are practical, and are founded on experiences long and corrected. Yes, but so are the dogmas about the supernatural with which we approach supernatural truth. It was to explain a tremendous experience that they arose.

Now, if I took these supernatural principles and compelled you to admit them before I allowed you to enter on physical research, you would say I was taking the principles of one kind of experience and forcing them on a quite different kind: that I was treating by the laws of one nature objects which have a very different nature—as if one were to test music by mathematics, or poetry by logic, or seek life's secret with a lamp and a lancet . . . You would be quite right if you spoke to me like this.

You will not wonder then if I want to apply your principle all round. The experience of nature (human or other) can never take the place of the religion (or, more correctly, of God.). You will be prepared now to hear me protest against the dogmatism with which you want to impose on my experience of the living God doctrines which you drew from the treatment of sensible nature. You want to subject the person of Christ entirely to methods which are very useful when you are testing natural processes or historical documents. But when you propose to apply rational principles as final to the Incarnation, you are taking it for granted that the Incarnation was, above all things, a rational process. Whereas it was in the nature of an act, and an act, being an act of will and personality, is beyond the rationality which explains a process. It was an experience of God's and therefore only to be met and owned by an experience of ours, i.e. not by a conviction or a conclusion, but by religion. The only real belief in the Incarnation is not assent but living faith.

If you propose to subject it to a human test, or reduce it to a philosophic process, you are as dogmatic as any Christian. You are worse, because you want to apply to my experience of faith principles and dogmas which you gathered in a different region outside faith. You are doing to religion what you fiercely resent that religion should do to art or science. You are limiting its freedom by foreign dogma.

Thus masterfully Forsyth upholds the autonomy of the Christian claim. Christian theology, as he construes it, is not an attempt to construct a 'Christian philosophy of life', complete and infallible. It is an attempt to explore the meaning of God's central act in Christ as it powerfully affects the life of the believer. The man who has never experienced this divine act in his own life has no rights to judge it by methods which, however valid in other fields, do not apply to the experienced fact of grace. In short, the Christian gospel cannot have anything else for its criterion. It is spiritually autonomous. If Christ is the only Son of God who has become incarnate, he stands in a different category from all other persons or things with which he might be compared. He is his own principle of interpretation. Life does not judge him; he judges life.

NOTES

1. S. J. Mikolaski in *Creative Minds in Contemporary Theology*, p. 310.

2. There is a short popular exposition in *RON*, pp. 9–22.

3. No more than Studdert-Kennedy did Forsyth shrink from what has been called the 'heresy' of Patripassianism.

4. *TGAA*, p. 85.

5. *POA*, p. 62.

6. *WOC*, p. 131.

7. *POA*, p. 149.

8. *JOG*, p. 47.

9. *PPMM*, p. 15.

10. *TGAA*, p. 173.

11. *Ibid*, p. 178.

12. This extract from *The Constructive Quarterly*, vol. 3, I owe to R. M. Brown, *P. T. Forsyth Prophet for To-day*, pp. 55f.

5

Sin and Salvation

What was Forsyth's purpose in all his theologizing? It was not to produce 'a new theology'. Only very naïve and ill-educated theologians (like R. J. Campbell) set out to do this. 'We stand in trust', said Forsyth, 'of a final revelation and whatever new thing awaits us, it must be a fresh ray from the old faith, and a fresh shoot from the old creed.' What he sought to give his generation was a renovated theology – the historic faith moralized, modernized, revitalized, a theology at once evangelical, experimental and ethical.

Nor did he aspire (like Tillich in our day) to be a system-maker, to write a *Summa Theologica*. To the rule that

> Our little systems have their day,
>
> They have their day and cease to be,

systematic theologies which undertake to comprehend the whole counsel of God are no exception. Nevertheless, Forsyth's writing is wonderfully unified by the presence in it of a few dominant ideas – like the holiness of God, the sinfulness of sin and the cruciality of the cross – so that, in the result, not many writers have fewer loose ends to their theological thinking than Forsyth.

Where should we begin our study of it? Forsyth defined the gospel as 'God's utmost with man's worst'. Accordingly the only right place to start is where Paul started his theological *magnum opus*, Romans, with 'the sin of man'. 'The truth of Christianity', said Forsyth,[1] 'must rest on a view of life which starts with the primacy and finality of the moral, recognizes the wreck of the moral, and presents the grand problem as the

56

restitution of the moral.' Only when we have diagnosed man's moral and spiritual disease can we properly understand God's remedy for it.

I

The Sin of Man

How did Forsyth conceive of sin and its fatal concomitant guilt? It was during that spiritual crisis which turned him from 'a Christian into a believer' that, as he said, 'God taught me what sin is and the theology of its cure.'[2] Doubtless in his 'liberal phase' he had regarded man as at heart good and seen sin (with the evolutionists) as a 'not yet' or (with the religious moralists) as a 'not now'. But 'when it pleased God' he said, 'by the revelation of his holiness and grace, to bring home his sin to him,' he came to see it as a 'no longer'. Sin is not a failure to live up to an ideal of human conduct which we have framed for ourselves, neither is it a crime – a transgression of the law of the state. Seen against the backdrop of eternity, it is rebellion against a holy God, so that, when we sin we are putting ourselves at a distance from God and creating a chasm between him and ourselves which we cannot, of our own efforts, bridge. Sin is radical alienation from the all-holy Father.

With the great theologians of the church down the centuries Forsyth held fast the dogma of 'original sin, the corruption of man's heart', regarded sin as a universal state which had helplessly infected not only the individual but the race. How this 'original sin' had first entered the world he was not minded to speculate. There it was in human nature as a stark, ineluctable reality and curse, and he was content to say:[3] 'The whole race is not only weighted with arrears, but infected with a blight. The train of history is not simply late, but there has been an accident due to malice and crime. We struggle not only with misfortune but with a curse.'

Like Niebuhr and others, he saw that sin is not a spiritual disease confined to isolated individuals of the race, whose infection others may escape. Sin is a *corporate* corruption. Like runners in the strawberry bed, we are all connected through a

57

common life-root, and through that root-system flows moral evil, sin. For to be human is to be caught up in the inherent egoism of society, to be involved in all the ambiguities of that situation, so that from the contagion of corporate sin only a complete 'drop-out' from society could hope to be immune. He saw too that there is no sin so subtle as the sin of goodness – the sin of the Pharisee of Christ's parable, the sin of 'the good people who do not know that they are not good'.

Moreover, the heart of sin is guilt. Unlike evil, which is a static concept, sin is something personal for which we are responsible – responsible to God. 'Against thee only have I sinned.' It is the holiness of the Almighty which turns sin into guilt, makes it personal, affects the conscience. Further, our sin is to be measured not so much by a law as by a person. As once in Galilee Peter had cried, 'Depart from me, for I am a sinful man, O Lord', so (said Forsyth) 'Christ came to reveal not only God but sin.'

The long and short of it all is that we men are deeply alienated from God, have forfeited the good relationship with God for which he designed us, and cannot, of ourselves, get out of dis-grace'[4] into grace.

The seriousness of sin, said Forsyth, is something we should never minimize. 'For God's sake do not tell poor prodigals and black scoundrels that they are better than they think,' he said,[4] 'for the conscience that is in hell is the first to be angered at ingenuities and futilities like these.' The Christian preacher must therefore ever deal faithfully with human sin. It was not the world's sorrow but its wickedness which broke Christ's heart. Therefore today the ambassador of Christ is called to condemn not only individual but social sin – the moral corruption in which we are all involved as members of society and for which each of us has a responsibility.

Sin expressing itself in guilt is the reality which must come home to us if ever we are to understand God's historic forgiveness and reconciliation in the cross. We must see sin as an affront to God's holiness, and ourselves – and our race – not simply as stray sheep or wandering prodigals but as rebels –

'rebels taken with weapons in our hands'. Accordingly, if we are to be forgiven by God and set on the road to 'newness of life', our first need is an existential realization of our condition.

But how is man to be brought to a proper sense of his own sin and guilt? Not, said Forsyth, by constantly flailing him with a sense of guilt. It was the vision of God's holiness which brought home to Isaiah his sinfulness. Therefore better far to show man the holiness of that God who by his very nature cannot palter with sin, and how in the gracious gift of his Son and the atoning cross he has judged sin and redeemed sinners.

Die sin must – or God, said Forsyth in his prophetic way. Heine's 'God will forgive me – that's his business,' he dismissed as sentimental trifling. A God of holy love cannot wink at sin, or waive it, but must judge it. God's judgment on sin is his wrath – the obverse side of his holy love. And to those who boggled at the idea that God could be angry with us, he replied that if God cares enough about us to be angry with us, he cares enough to redeem us. 'The love of God is not more real than the wrath of God. For he can be really angry only with those he loves. And how can Absolute Love love without acting to save?'[5]

II

But the Grace of God in the Cross

For Forsyth, the cross was the pivot on which Christianity turned. (Here he found the Reformers right, the creed-makers wrong. The Reformers put the cross where the New Testament puts it – at the centre. The creed-makers mention it only in passing. But 'the cross and not the cradle holds the secret of the Lord', and any true Christianity must restore the cross to the position it held in the mind of Christ and in the 'tradition' of the church from the earliest days – *vide* I Cor. 15.3.)

In Forsyth's view, the cross was not a mere 'life-saving apparatus for personal escape', neither was it a mere exhibition of God's love. It was an act of God in Christ which effected in principle the redemption of the race. In the cross God intervened as the world's Saviour, not in spite of his own holiness but because of it. At the cost of his own sacrifice he honoured his own holiness. On the other hand, at the cross, Christ, as man's representative, confessed God's holiness while undergoing sin's judgment, and reconciled guilty man to holy God. 'A holy God self-atoned in Christ', said Forsyth summing up his view,[6] 'is the moral centre of the sinful world. Our justification has its key in God's justification of himself.' The cross was thus the reconciliation in history whereby God's kingdom was set up, as it was the pledge of that kingdom yet to be consummated beyond history, for this world is not big enough to contain the whole of God's eschatology.

Now to elucidate this summary in some detail. Forsyth did not refurbish any one historical doctrine of atonement. (Rather he sought to bring together the three aspects of Christ's work on which different theologians have fastened down the centuries – the cross as victory, as satisfaction and as regeneration.) He rejected this or that view held by the doctors of the church. He said we must never think of grace as procured by the atonement, or imagine Christ as offering an equivalent for our punishment, or talk of a transfer of guilt as if it were a ledger amount which could be shifted by divine finance.

As we approach his positive teaching, let us note two things. First, if there is any one single New Testament passage which sheds special light on the meaning of the cross, it is II Cor. 5.14–6.2. Here Paul describes the *end* of Christ's work as 'reconciliation' and its *means* as atonement, since 'God was in Christ reconciling the world to himself' is followed by 'not counting their trespasses' and 'God made him to be sin for us who knew no sin'. ('Atonement', he explains, is the covering of sin by something which God himself provided, and so its covering by God himself. 'Reconciliation' is the total result of Christ's work in permanently changing the relation between God and man from hostility to peace.)

Second: we shall never understand Forsyth till we take as seriously as he did the holiness of God – his moral majesty, his absolute goodness. Christians, losing touch with the God of the Bible whose majesty is as his mercy, had taken to construing his love in purely sentimental ways. So, like Heine, they had turned the problem of divine forgiveness into a matter of easy indulgence. But, protested Forsyth, the essence of God's love is its awful purity, a purity which cannot traffic with sin but must judge it. If we are to think rightly about God, we must think of him as the holy Father who loves all his children with a seeking love; but it is a love which, though it desires nothing but the responsive love of his children, must deal exigently with human sin, and is inexorable against evil.

Here then is the problem: on the one hand, the sin of man; on the other, the holiness of God. How are these two to be reconciled? Plainly we sinners cannot, of ourselves, atone. If we could, we should be, as Luther said, 'the proudest jackasses under heaven'. To right the wrongness between God and man, what is needed is an act of reparation to God's holiness which will alter the whole relationship between them and repair the broken fellowship, the sundered communion: an act of God himself: in fact, the act of the cross. Forsyth sums up[7] the problem and its solution thus: 'The Holy Father's first care is holiness. The first charge on a Redeemer is satisfaction to that holiness. The Holy Father is one who does and must atone. As Holy Father he offers a sacrifice rent from his own heart. It is made to him by no third party, but by himself in his Son, and it is made to no foreign power but to his own holy nature and law.'

Here, then in the idea of an offering made by God to man, and not by man to God, is what is called an *objective* doctrine of atonement. And out goes any suggestion of Christ acting as a 'daysman', i.e. one who in a dispute puts one hand on one head and the other on another and brings two persons together.

If Forsyth taught an objective doctrine of atonement, he saw the cross in its *double* character – as an act of God and as an act done in humanity. If he stressed the first, as he did, he only does what scripture does. Moreover, by so doing he avoided two errors that had vitiated earlier doctrines of atonement: (1) the concept of the atonement as the appeasement of an angry God by a loving Christ; and (2) the destruction of the moral unity of the Godhead.

Accordingly, while he can speak of Christ's dealing with the

Father in his work, Forsyth speaks mostly of this work as one that only God can do.

Christ's dealing with the Father (to take it first) was, like an iceberg, largely hidden: 'The great thing was done with God. It was independent of our knowledge of it. The greatest thing ever done in the world was done out of it . . . The most ever done for us was done behind our backs . . . Doing this *for* us was the first condition of doing anything *with* us.'[8]

What then has he to say of the atonement as God's act? The cross is an atonement made to God's holiness – made by God himself. Who covered the sin of man? The all-seeing God himself. The atonement was not made to God but by God. The real objective element is that God made the atonement and gave it finished to man.

Two moral elements lie at the heart of what God did in Christ to establish his holiness. They are (1) obedience and (2) judgment. 'What Christ presented to God for his complete joy and satisfaction was a perfect racial obedience.'[9] Whether in the Old Testament or the New, obedience is the truth of sacrifice. In the work God gave his Son to do – the sacrificial shedding of his blood – Christ made a complete sacrifice of his will – that will which 'is our ownest own, the only and dear thing we can and really ought to sacrifice'. And the satisfying thing to the holy Father was not an equivalent penalty – as if God were a great Shylock demanding his pound of flesh – but his Son's holy obedience.

Next, judgment. Because God is holy, he must deal faithfully with men's sins. The cross shows him doing just this. 'Him who knew no sin,' says Paul, 'God made to be sin for us' in order that we might become one with the goodness of God himself. Christ experienced sin as God does, while he experienced its effects as man does. 'There is a penalty and curse for sin, and Christ consented to enter that region.'[10] (We think of the agony in Gethsemane and of the cry of dereliction – that dereliction which was 'the real descent into hell.') 'God did not punish Christ,' says Forsyth, 'but Christ entered the dark shadow of God's penalty upon sin.'[11]

Nor was his role merely passive. From within the sphere of sin's penalty he actively confessed God's holiness. Not with his lips alone but with his whole life and death. He did justice to God's holiness by confessing it with a holiness equal to the Father's own, so making possible the forgiveness of a world which could only be achieved by judgment.

(Here some will find morally repulsive the doctrine that God judged sin on the head of the sinless Christ. But is there not a solution to their difficulty – the judgment of the sinless for the guilty – in the distinction between personal and corporate sin? Personally, Jesus was sinless, but such was his solidarity with humanity – so irrevocably had he betrothed himself to the human race for better, for worse – that he was able to share in its *corporate* sin and so submit to God's judgment upon it.)

How then does all this affect us sinners? Directly and deeply because in his sacrifice Christ, 'a public person', acted as the race's representative. Not by the will of man choosing Christ but by the will of Christ choosing man and freely identifying himself with him. So, from the midst of the fires of judgment (says Forsyth) there came from Christ, on man's behalf, a solidary confession of God's holiness.

What then is the fruit of the atonement? A world's reconciliation, as Paul says. What Christ saved was the human race, and we are each of us, saved in a social salvation. But is the world's reconciliation really accomplished, without all men repenting and putting their trust in Christ for time and eternity? Yes, in principle. The thing is done, it is not to do. 'The Cross of Christ was the world's great day of judgment, the crisis of all crises' (Cf. John 12.30, 'Now is the judgment of this world').[12] What remains is to follow it up, actualize it, appropriate it.

Here we reach an important element in Forsyth's teaching – what may be called his 'prospective view' of the atonement. Our holiness, he says, was latent in Christ's who alone could and must create it. Christ is the pledge not only of God's holy love to us but also of our response to it by a total change of will and life. Thus the living Christ prolongs his work in the New

Humanity – that complete and colossal Man Paul speaks of in Ephesians – which he creates. When you think of what Christ did for the race, Forsyth says, never forget our living communion with him. Think then of that historic reconciliation of his being worked out to cover the whole of history and to enter each soul through the Spirit.

Before us rises a picture of Christ presenting along with his own holy obedience the penitent love he is yet to create in his people, and of the almighty Father accepting not only him but us in him and with him, – accepted (as Paul would say) in the beloved. So we are left with the vision of a God whose majesty is as his mercy, and whose omnipotence is chiefly shown in forgiving, redeeming and settling all souls in worship in the temple of a new heaven and a new earth full of holiness.

III

Therefore Newness of Life

To God's grace redemptively revealed in the cross the only proper response on the part of sinful man is *faith*. Faith, which is the gift of God and the work of the Holy Spirit, means taking God at his living and redeeming Word in Christ crucified and risen. It is not the act of a moment only but the attitude of a whole life. It is 'the grand venture in which we commit our whole soul and future to the confidence that Christ is not an illusion but the reality of God.'[13] To make that 'grand venture' is the first step on the road to salvation. For when God forgives us for Christ's sake, the same act which disburdens us of our guilt and brings us peace with God (which is 'not glassy calm but mighty confidence'), not only places us in a new community, the church, but sets our life in another key than the natural. Christ becomes our power as well as our comfort, and we exult in hope of the glory of God.

This is the work of the Holy Spirit whose role it is to convey to us the virtue of 'the finished work of Christ'. The witness of the Spirit in our hearts is 'Christ's perpetual interpretation of his own work as gospel. The Spirit lights the Bible, leads the church, anoints the ministry, and all by a constant rejuvenation of the gospel and its power to create, criticize and create anew.'[14]

Regeneration, or sanctification – not in individual lives only but collectively in the church's life in the world – is thus the true work of that 'other Paraclete' (or 'Standby') as John calls the Spirit. But, alas, said Forsyth, we modern Christians have sadly debased and misconstrued the meaning of that grand old word 'sanctification'. In our modern man-centred religion, we have turned it into self-consecration. But sanctification is not spiritual self-culture, and 'it is a dangerous thing to work at your own holiness'.[15] Paul did not consecrate himself to his great work. He obeyed a call and found his sanctification – his growth in grace – in the pursuit of his ministry. So we too are sanctified when we are on our Saviour's business. Growth in grace comes not by working at it but by passing ever more deeply into self-forgetfulness – into the grace, the cross and the service of Christ.

Sanctification is thus but a maturer faith in our justification, or forgiveness, by God in Christ and a deeper life in our Justifier.

Such is Forsyth's account of sin and salvation. Some of the language he uses suggests the Puritan divines now largely discredited and forgotten. Freely he concedes that the old divines' presentation of sin and salvation can never again appeal to men today. Yet, he insists, the spiritual verities for which they stood – the soul's own civil war, man's sullen severance from God, his ostrich hope of escaping God's law and – on the other hand – the free but costly forgiveness of God wrought once for all on the cross and for the race, and now brought home to men by the Holy Spirit – these remain as true as ever, provided we can moralize and modernize them – preach them in contemporary thought-form and idiom.

What we need today is 'a positive Gospel', said Forsyth. In one of his greatest books he spelt out in detail what he meant by that phrase. But compelled to sum it up, he defined it in four phrases:[16]

(1) God has fully and finally forgiven us;

(2) He has done so for Christ's sake;

(3) Every other article of Christian faith flows from this;

(4) Every energy of the moral life has this as its source and standard.

Such a gospel, if it is *au fait* with modern man's spiritual malaise and expresses itself in ways he can understand, can yet speak to the condition of twentieth-century man in his sin-sickness and spiritual bewilderment. It is we, Christ's heralds today, who are timid and unsure. But God has yet more light and truth to break forth from that Word which he spoke for man's redeeming in Christ's cross and resurrection, and though

> The centuries go gliding,
> Yet still we have abiding
> With us that Spirit Holy
> To make us brave and lowly.

Our stricken world needs that light and truth, as the Spirit waits to take it home to all men ready to make 'the grand venture' of Christian faith. Get you to the proclaiming of it, you servants of the Word! This is Forsyth's call to Christ's ministers today.

NOTES

1. *TGAA*, p. 107.
2. *Christian World Pulpit*, 21 March 1906, p 186.
3. *TGAA*, p. 174.
4. *PPMM*, p. 154.
5. *WOC*, p. 190.
6. *JOG*, p. 94.
7. *GHF*, p. 4.
8. *Ibid*, p. 19.
9. *WOC*, p. 118.
10. *Ibid*, p. 128.
11. *PPMM*, p. 361.

12. *WOC*, p. 119.
13. *PPJC*, p. 205.
14. *CGS*, p. 91.
15. *WOC*, p. 80. Cf. *TGAA*, p. 161: 'Seek first for the Kingdom and sanctification will be added; care for Christ and he will take care of your soul; sail by the Cross and you will sail into holiness.'
16. *London Quarterly Review*, January 1904, p. 68.

6

The Person of the Saviour

Christ's *work* is the master-key to his *person*. What then should we think and say of one who has done for us what Christ has done? In *The Person and Place of Jesus Christ* Forsyth gives us his answer to this question – and his greatest book.

To understand what a portent it was, we should remember when it was written. The year was 1909. It was a time when theological liberalism was at its apogee, and every attempt was being made to accommodate Christianity to modern thought. Quite the worst of these attempts was R. J. Campbell's 'New Theology' given to the world two years before. It blurred all distinctions between God and man, played down the reality of evil and sin, and, holding every man to be 'a potential Christ,' declared, 'Jesus is God, but so are we.'

Though Forsyth does not name Campbell, he had him in mind when, in approving a need for the restatement of Christian doctrine, he insisted that it must be done 'by competent and reverent people, not by amateurs with but a natural religion and a poor education, or none, on the subject; for the worst heresy is quackery'.[1]

But if all liberals did not descend to Campbell's wild and woolly pantheism, Forsyth in his book was consciously going 'against the stream', so that in 1909 there were few to appraise it at its true greatness. To be sure, H. R. Mackintosh in his book on the *Person of Jesus Christ* (1912) discerned the originality and power of Forsyth's volume; but it had to wait till 1925 for a just verdict on its worth. It came not from a Nonconformist but from the Anglican, J. K. Mozley:[2] Work of real greatness in the field of christology, he said, is very rare. Seldom does one feel that the writer has measured the solemn grandeur of his subject and has treated of it, according to its scale. But just this Forsyth has done. He has put into it all the best of which he was capable, and the result is 'something equally impressive as religion and as theology'; in short, 'a great book'.

This, and the fact that the argument really marches, are the secrets of its greatness. 'The writer chases no hares,' wrote Lovell Cocks,[3] 'stoops to pick up no golden apples, but runs swiftly and surely to his goal.'

After an opening reveille, the book falls into three parts which Forsyth, in military metaphors, calls: Reconnaissance, Advance, and Advance in Force.

I

Reconnaissance

Sixty years ago, everywhere liberals of one kind or another were inviting men to believe *with* Christ rather than to believe *in* him; to replace the gospel of Christ with the religion of Jesus. It sounds all so plausible, modern and attractive – till you begin to study the New Testament evidence with the scholars' help. Then you learn that there never was a time, even in the earliest church, when Christianity meant the religion of Jesus which you are being asked to accept. But the German 'religious-historical' school, to whom chiefly we owe this discovery, are themselves no better. They invite us to see in Christ 'a splendid column of spray set up by the collision of east and west',[4] and to venerate him as a sublime symbol of aspiring and ascending man. So they allow the idea of evolution to make havoc of their Christian thinking. They utterly fail to comprehend the magnitude of the Christ who made the church and produced the New Testament. 'In Christ God did not simply countersign the best intuitions of the human heart, but he created a new heart within us.'[5] In short, the tendency of this brave new version of Christianity is backwards. Like

Molière's ghost (says Forsyth) it has improved very much for the worse!

How then are we to explain Christ's greatness – a greatness which the scholars' re-discovery of the true meaning of the eschatology of the Gospels serves only to enhance? 'The spiritual power which broke up the old pagan world and founded a new', said Forsyth,[6] 'is here, in Christ, compressed to a single volcanic point.' What a truly sovereign master of men and events is the Person who fills the Gospels! What a super-human sense of authority is here conjoined with a super-human sense of humility! But Forsyth's portrait of the Christ of the Gospels deserves to be described in his own words:[7]

Lord of himself and all besides; with an irresistible power to force, and even hurry, events on a world scale; and yet with the soul that sat among children, and the heart in which children sat. He had an intense reverence for the past that was yet too small for him. It rent him to rend it, and yet he had to break it up, to the breaking of his own heart, in the greatest revolution the world ever saw. He was an austere man, a severe critic, a born fighter, of choleric wrath and fiery scorn, so that the people thought he was Elijah or the Baptist: yet he was gentle to the last degree, especially with those ignorant and out of the way. In the thick of life and love he yet stood detached, sympathetic yet aloof, cleaving at once to men and to solitude.

With an almost sacramental idea of human relations, especially the central relation of marriage, he yet avoided for himself every bond of property, vocation, or family; and he cut those bonds when they stood between men and himself . . . With a royal and almost proud, sense of himself, he poured out his soul unto God and unto death and was the friend of publicans and sinners.

Such is the Figure who dominates the Gospels. Inevitably we ask: Is Godhead necessary to explain this Figure – yes, and his impact on history, and his effect on the human soul?

Yet, great as Christ's personality was, the real site of his greatness lies in what he *did*, in the cross where the real

Jesus at last took effect, crowning and consummating the work his Father had given him to do.

How then are we to construe his connection with the Deity? Down the centuries men have reacted in three ways to the mystery of Christ. The Socinians (or Unitarians) have seen in him prophet and hero, the classic instance of created man. The spiritual successors of Arius have found in him God's plenipotentiary – the superman, a half-god but still a creature. The Athanasians have confessed in him Immanuel, God with us, the Supernal Man, the Lord from heaven.

Still today the lay type of mind is attracted by Socinianism. Arianism has a following among those not content with a thin Unitarianism. But does not Arianism fall short of what the evangelical experience demands? Could God's plenipotentiary, for the last purposes of the soul and race, still be a creature? Could the sinner's reconcilement with a holy God be effected by anyone less than God?

These questions close the reconnaisance. We are ready now for –

II

The Advance

Here the first question is, *Was Christ a part of his gospel?* The apostles – and indeed modern scholarship as a whole – say that he was. Our clever modern scholars say he was not. Who is right? The apostles? Or the liberals?

Suppose we appeal to the Synoptic Gospels. Do they indeed, as the liberals allege, yield us no more than 'a preacher of the Father', a figure who has no real place in the gospel he proclaims? On the contrary, they show us One who declared that Israel, the supreme organ of God's will on earth, would be wrecked on its attitude to himself; One who promised a supreme blessing to all those ready to lose life for his sake and the gospel's; One who solemnly affirmed that on men's acceptance or rejection of himself their eternal destiny would depend; One whose claim to be central to his own gospel and to be the sole

71

mediator between God and man comes to supreme expression in Matt. 11.27:

> All things have been delivered to me by my Father;
> And no one knows the Son except the Father;
> And no one knows the Father except the Son,
> And any one to whom the Son chooses to reveal him.

Nor is this all. The great thing that Jesus brought to the world was not a doctrine but a deed, a deed not finished till he died. And the claim of Jesus in his cross and resurrection is greater than any explicit in his mouth during his ministry.

We cannot therefore allow the critics to repudiate the New Testament version of Christ for one of their own making. They have no right to say that, if we wish to find Christ's Christianity, we must confine ourselves to the words of Jesus. These do not give us the complete Christ. It needs the whole New Testament – and not only certain sayings of Jesus critically sifted from the Synoptic Gospels – to show us who Christ is.

So let us turn to *the apostles' testimony about Christ* in the epistles. Is it a true interpretation of him? What is their place, if any, in the economy of revelation? The question we have to answer is: Granted that God revealed himself in Christ, is the apostolic record of it just man construing, so that the apostles' witness is no more authoritative than the reflection of any later Christians?

Let us (says Forsyth) distinguish between the material and the formal revelation. In the material sense Christ was the final revelation of God: in him God spoke, God acted. But this material revelation remained incomplete till it was consummated formally in the interpretation. As a lesson is not rightly taught until it is learnt, so Christ's finished work was not really finished until it was got home. Therefore when it is asked, why did Christ not explain himself and his work more fully? the answer is that he did – *when his work was done*. But where? In the apostles, through the Spirit. This is precisely Paul's theme in I Cor. 2 – a passage classic for the psychology of apostolic inspiration and its abiding value.

Now we may see the apostles' true place in the economy of revelation. We are not in the same position as they. They were unique. But their uniqueness is not constituted merely by their historical position, though we must give due weight to the fact that they were eye-witnesses. What did they see? Not mere events but a Person whose self-manifestation they accepted by faith. And what they give us is not primarily their own personal reactions but what they received from the living Christ, i.e. revelation. The epistles are not the reflections of religious geniuses. The testimony embodied in them is the authentic teaching of their risen and regnant Lord, through the Spirit, guiding them into all the truth of the gospel.

Yet we cannot leave this matter with the proof that Christ was central to the gospel he proclaimed and the claim that in the apostles he interpreted his finished work, through the Spirit. We must also lay our account with the testimony to Christ's saviourhood given by countless Christians down nineteen centuries. What is it worth?

Today, in the quest for truth, no argument so appeals to people as that from experience. Now in Christianity this means experience of Christ; for what nature is to the scientist that Christ is to faith. Yet many modern scholars – expert indeed in the techniques of their craft but with little experience of real life, men living in the shelter of academic bowers who have never known the spiritual slums – warn us solemnly against relying on this very argument.

'What! [cries Forsyth] Am I really forbidden to make any use of my personal experience of Christ for the purposes even of scientific theology? Should it make no difference to the evidence for Christ's Resurrection that I have had personal dealings with the risen Christ as my Saviour, nearer and dearer than my own flesh and blood? Is his personal gift of forgiveness to me, in the central experience of my life, of no value in settling the objective value of his Cross and Person?

No, murmur these cloistered critics, of no value objectively and scientifically. If you claim to commune with Christ, you must never gird at those who traffic with saints. There is no real difference between our experience of a saint and our experience of the Saviour. How does Forsyth answer these critics?

First, in *personal* terms, thus: If I am not to doubt absolutely everything, I must find my practical certainty in that which founds my moral life – especially my *new* moral life. And this is Christ. What I have in him is not a fleeting impression but a life change. In my inmost experience, tested through long years, he has brought me God – has been Immanuel to me. Therefore if you doubt the validity of my experience, you must do it on the ground of something deeper and surer than the certainty my experience gives me. And there is none. There is no rational certainty which has a right to challenge the moral – and especially the moral certainty of being saved.

But to the suggestion that there is no difference between experience of a Saviour and experience of a saint there is a second answer, this time in historical terms. It is this. Christ has entered history with such a piercing, crucial moral effect as no saint has ever done. And he has entered the life of the whole church no less than that of the individual: 'I know him, and the Church knows him, as a person of infinite power to create fresh experience of himself, which is experience of God. My contact with him by faith is continually deepening my experience of him. And, as my experience deepens, it brings home a Christ objective in history, and creative of the experience, and the life, and the deeds of a whole vast Church, meant, and moving, to subdue mankind not to itself, but to the faith of the gospel.'[9]

So, to the question: Can my individual experience give absolute truth? The answer is: (1) My experienced salvation is not a passing impression but a life faith; and (2) standing over my experience is the whole experience of the evangelical succession down the centuries:

> I asked them whence their victory came.
> They, with united breath,
> Ascribed their conquest to the Lamb,
> Their triumph to his death.

The repeated emphasis, in this whole argument, on the moral prepares the way for the second parallel of 'the Advance' – what Forsyth calls 'the moralizing of dogma'. 'Morality is the nature of things,' said Butler. Yes, says Forsyth, and as the moral is the real, and as the movements of the Supreme Reality are morally revealed, so must they be morally interpreted. Therefore all Christian dogma – whether it be the omnipotence of God or the absoluteness of Christ – must be expressed in moral and personal terms. This must apply, above all, to the doctrine of the incarnation. Since admittedly it was for a moral purpose – to save sinners – its nature must be moral, and morally it must be interpreted.

Long ago, at Chalcedon (AD 451), men sought to explain the incarnation not in moral but in intellectual terms – terms of pure being and substance. They spoke of a union of two Natures in one Person. Such 'Chalcedonism' (and it still survives) savours too much of mystic theosophy. Its categories are elemental and physical. It views the union of the two Natures in Christ as an act of might – an act which united the Natures *into* a Person rather than *through* a Person, an act more magical than moral.

Such categories, based on an outmoded Hellenic philosophy, no longer carry conviction. Whatever the Reformation did, it compelled us to think of salvation in moral and religious ways. And the categories which come home to modern man (as they are deep rooted in the New Testament) are those which speak in personal terms and lay the stress on religious experience. Therefore nowadays we must do our thinking about Christ's person in moral terms.

What happens if we do so? We seem to be shut up to one of two views. Either we see the incarnation as the fruit of a grand moral act of Christ in heaven before he entered the world (this implies a *kenōsis*;) or we see it as a continuous and ascending moral achievement in Christ's earthly life wherein his moral growth, always in unbroken union with his Father, gave but growing effect to God's indwelling – an indwelling which culminated in the cross and resurrection and finally identified

75

him with God. You may call the first view that of 'progressive incarnation', the second that of 'progressive deification.' But must we really choose between the two? If you combine them, says Forsyth, you may get much nearer the truth about Christ, and what you will get is a moral rather than a magical miracle.

The general advance by two parallels is over. We are ready now for the Final Advance – the full Forsythian doctrine of Christ's person.

III

Advance in Force

How boldly Forsyth begins his final push! He insists at once that One who, by common Christian consent, has an *epilogue* of eternal history must have had a *prologue* of the same. In other words, to explain the finality of Christ, we must believe, as the early church did, in *the pre-existence* of Christ.

Nothing less than this belief will explain the sonship of such a passage as Matt. 11.27. Whereas 'of no other person can it be said that his relation to God constitutes his personality, yet in Christ's case the whole relation to the Father, namely, sonship, did constitute that personality. Think it away and nothing is left'.[10]

More: nothing less than this belief will carry the fulness of the church's adoring faith, her organ voice of liturgy in every age (as in the *Te Deum*). Paul, who had found in Christ the sovereign power and grace of the Almighty himself, could not believe that his story really began in a Bethlehem cradle. No more can we evade 'the retrospective pressure' of our faith in him. With Paul, Peter, the Writer to the Hebrews and the Seer of Patmos we are driven to regard Christ's earthly life as the obverse of a previous heavenly one. There was an act of renunciation outside the walls of the world and the Son's sacrifice began before he entered it.

All this implies a doctrine of *kenōsis*, or 'self-emptying', on Christ's part; and, as every student of theology knows, men like William Temple and Donald Baillie, have boggled at the doctrine. Observe then how our *maestro* meets the common objections to it.

The doctrine is incompatible, say some, with the changelessness of God. The only immutable thing in God, counters Forsyth, is his holy love, and this cannot be immobile. *Infinitum capax finiti* is what the Christian faith affirms: the infinite God must be capable of infinite self-determination, for an Infinite which could not reduce itself to the finite world, would, by that very inability, be reduced to finitude.

The doctrine, others object, means that Christ, in becoming man, parted with his divine attributes. And how – supposing this to be possible – can a divine Being do this and remain divine? This, replies Forsyth, is not my conception of *kenōsis*. What we ought to say is that the attributes were retracted into a different mode of being – from being actual, they became potential. What we should see in the incarnate Christ is 'a Godhead self-reduced but real whose infinite power took effect in self-humiliation'; and what the *kenōsis* really means is that 'the Son by an act of love's omnipotence set aside the style of a God and took the style of a servant, and the mode of action that marks human nature' (Cf. Phil. 2.6–11).[11]

Nothing could better show what Forsyth means by 'the moralizing of dogma'. The great moral act in the heavens becomes the fontal principle of the incarnation. But more: such a view leaves us untroubled by the limitations and ignorance of the incarnate Christ. He consented not to know, and he was mighty not to do. (Here, to help understanding, Forsyth uses the analogy of the university student with a bent for philosophy who, on his father's death, has to take over the family business, renounce his intellectual interests and forget most of what he once knew.)

But Forsyth gives us much more than an improved doctrine of *kenōsis*. To explain the incarnate life he uses not only the idea of *kenōsis* but also that of *plērōsis*. A Christ merely 'kenotic' is not enough. All we get thus is a humbled God. But we need also a royal and redeeming one. Therefore hand in hand with *kenōsis*, or self-emptying, there must go *plērōsis* or self-fulfilment.

Consider it this way. In man's religious experience we can trace two vertical and personal movements: God seeking man, and man in his turn responding obediently to that revelation. Now transfer all this to Christ. Think of his person in terms not of a union of two natures (as they did at Chalcedon) but of a union of these two personal movements. In the historic life of Christ the two movements – perfect revelation and perfect religion – were united, involuted. Alongside the *diminuendo* of *kenōsis* there went a corresponding *crescendo* of *plērōsis*. As Christ's personal history enlarged and ripened by every experience, and as he was always found equal to every moral crisis, the latent Godhead became more and more mighty as his life's interior. As his personality grew in depth and scope, it asserted itself with more power. The more Christ laid down his personal life, the more he gained his divine soul. He worked out the salvation he was, and moved by his history *to* that supernatural world *in* which he moved by his nature. And the life culminated in the perfection of his own soul and of our salvation in the cross, the resurrection and the glory.

Thus, in Forsyth's view, the story of Christ's incarnate life of growth becomes the story of his recovery, by moral conquest, of that mode of being from which, by a tremendous moral act, he came. This is *plērōsis*. The whole doctrine of Christ's person seems to us to accord well with what may have been the earliest Christian hymn ever written (Phil. 2.6–11). Not only so, but it does full justice to the moral side of Christ's human life. Though his relation to his Father was always immediate and unbroken (cf. John 3.13 'The Son of man whose home is in heaven'), he had yet no immunity from the moral law that we must earn our greatest legacies and by toil and conflict appropriate our best gifts.

IV

How shall we appraise Forsyth's *magnum opus*? Some have said that Forsyth had no real interest in the incarnation *by itself*. Does he not declare that the heart of the gospel for him is 'the Son made sin' rather than 'the Word made flesh'? Of course he does, and we can understand why. Ever since Chalcedon the tendency has been to conceive the incarnation in metaphysical rather than in moral terms. Bold, even paradoxical, statements like these by Forsyth are, if you like, dictated by polemical necessities: he must at all costs, in the interest of Christian truth, wean men from outmoded ways of thinking and lay the emphasis where it should be laid. In some circles the doctrine of the atonement had been displaced from the centre by the doctrine of the incarnation. 'Harm has been done,' said Mandell Creighton,[12] 'by the prominence given in our day to the doctrine of the Incarnation over the doctrine of the Atonement. It weakens the sense of sin, which is one of the greatest bulwarks against unbelief, and through which we live into a larger world'. In this, said Forsyth, Creighton showed more insight than Westcott. And if he protested against this tendency, had he not every right to do so? Had he not the main burden of the New Testament at his back? 'Not Bethlehem but Calvary is the focus of revelation', rightly said James Denney.[13] Besides, when men say Forsyth could not appreciate the full glory of the incarnation is there not a sufficient answer in Forsyth's own book where the moral splendour of the Son's self-emptying is set forth with a power that even Westcott would have gratefully acknowledged?

Again, it is charged that Forsyth's own christology confronts us with a paradox no less tremendous than that of the Chalcedonian formula about the two natures. How can we have united in one historic personality absolute God and relative man? How can there be brought together absolute grace and growth in grace, a victory won and a victory still to win? These are fair questions. Let it therefore be granted that Forsyth does not remove the paradox. Yet let it also be claimed that as he states it in moral and personal terms and grounds it on evangelical experience of Christ, it is at once more faithful to the New Testament and much more intelligible to modern man. For the solution which he offers is of 'God's Word to man' and 'man's word to God' – perfect revelation and perfect religion – interpenetrating in one Person.

This is 'moralized' theology. Not an alternative to Chalcedonian christology, for Forsyth never contested the truth for which the men of Chalcedon stood – but a more luminous, a more realistic, more satisfying attempt to irradiate the ultimate mystery of how God became a human being. If this is orthodoxy, it is *vital* orthodoxy. Too often orthodox discussions of Christ's person suffer from theological arterio-sclerosis. Anything less 'sclerotic' than Forsyth's treatment of the problem could not be imagined. Here is a doctrine which does full justice to the moral miracle of the God-man. In Christ we are bidden to see One who, for love of sinful man, renounced the high glories of heaven to become man, taking a servant's form, and who by his life of perfect obedience to his heavenly Father, even unto death on the cross, gained for himself the highest place that heaven affords. In Christ we have not the whole range of God but the whole heart of him, and of his story we can say:

> What lacks then of perfection fit for God
> But just the instance which this tale supplies
> Of love without a limit? So is strength,
> So is intelligence; let love be so,
> Unlimited in its self-sacrifice,
> Then is the tale true and God shows complete.

And if to some Forsyth's christology may seem here and there to be super-subtle, dull must the Christian be of soul who is not moved by Forsyth's personal confession: 'I should count a life well spent, and the world well lost, if, after tasting all its experiences, and facing all its problems, I had no more to show at its close, or carry with me to another life, than the acquisition of a real, sure, humble and grateful faith in the eternal and incarnate Son of God.'[14]

Is it not the abiding merit of Forsyth's masterpiece that he has made it easier for others to make that faith their own?

NOTES

1. *PPJC*, p. 87.
2. *The Heart of the Gospel*, p. 87.
3. *The Expository Times*, April 1953, p. 195.
4. *PPJC*, p. 42.
5. *Ibid*, p. 58.
6. *Ibid*, p. 64.
7. *Ibid*, pp. 65f.
8. *Ibid*, p. 196.
9. *Ibid*, p. 203.
10. *Ibid*, p. 285.
11. *Ibid*, p. 307.
12. *CGS*, pp. 119f.
13. *The Death of Christ*, p. 325. Denney adds: 'The New Testament knows nothing of an Incarnation which can be defined apart from its relation to atonement; it is to put away sin, and to destroy the works of the devil, that even in the evangelist of the Incarnation the Son of God is made manifest.'
14. *PPJC*, p. 55.

7

Church and Sacraments

From the person of Christ we turn now to what Forsyth has to say about his body, the church, with its two sacraments of baptism and the Lord's supper.

I

His *Church and Sacraments* appeared in 1917. To appreciate how 'modern' he is in this book, we need to remember how sadly in eclipse the doctrine of the church was, in some circles, when he was writing. On the one hand, liberal Protestantism in the first two decades of the century refused to take seriously the idea of the church and its place in Christianity. Radical scholars were blandly assuring their readers that Jesus never intended a church. On the other hand, many evangelical Christians were commonly heard to say, 'Give us more Christianity and less Churchianity' as if church and gospel were complete incompatibles.

Now, as every student knows, there has been an entire *volte face* by our learned men, as witness the steady stream of books from R. N. Flew's *Jesus and His Church* to Anders Nygren's *Christ and His Church*, to name only two. Our scholars and theologians have now decided not only that Jesus intended to create a new people of God, but that the church is an integral part of God's saving work in Christ as the New Testament understands it. In fact, the rediscovery of the church's role in early Christianity has been hailed by Anton Fridrichsen as the greatest event in the exegetical science of our generation.[1]

But all this was no 'discovery' to Forsyth. He was as convinced as S. J. Stone that

The church's one foundation
Is Jesus Christ her Lord

though he characteristically amended, 'not Christ simply but Christ crucified and atoning'. He had no doubt that the creation of a new people of God was the purpose of that work which Jesus consummated on the cross, and that in the New Testament epistles the same act which sets us 'in Christ' sets us also in his church.[2]

Let us summarize his findings. First, the church is the result of God's historic action in Christ. Differing from every kind of club or voluntary association, it is a creation of God, not a compact of men. It is of the very *esse* of Christianity. Religion could go on without a church; Christianity could not. His other certainty was that 'the church was one before it was many.'[3] Earlier scholars like Hatch had argued that the various early Christian communities were originally local and independent associations which later coalesced to form a confederation – the church of Christ. Not so, said Forsyth, originally it was one as the *vis-à-vis* of the one Redeemer. Study the New Testament, he said, and you will find that in apostolic times the local congregation was the outcrop, or outpost, of the one church or people of God. It was not the empirical agglutination of many local congregations but their *prius*. The church was born one. The total church was spiritually prior to the local. And what apostles like Paul planted was not churches but stations of the one great church, microcosms of a macrocosm. Of course Forsyth was right in this – see K. L. Schmidt's article on *ecclēsia* in Gerhard Kittel's *Theological Dictionary of the New Testament* – but in the atomic individualism of his day it was a truth not commonly apprehended.

How did Forsyth conceive the church's vocation under God? It was called to be God's 'collective missionary to the world.'[4] Its business was to evangelize the nations, consecrate those thus evangelized, and help and heal those who were ignorant and out of the way. What made the church, he held, was really the cross. Old Israel had been called to world-mission. The promise to Abraham had been 'in thy seed all the nations of the earth be blessed'. Isaiah had declared that as God's servant Israel was to be 'a light to lighten the gentiles'. But in the supreme crisis of her history, when 'God's own apostle' came to his own people, Israel made its fatal refusal of Christ, failed to see its real vocation and destiny in him. So he who was Israel's crowning soul became its final doom, and old Israel's work passed to a new nation, a landless nation, a universal nation, a spiritual Israel united by the blood not of Abraham but of Christ, the true Messiah of Israel and the Saviour of men.

In Christ's death, Paul tells us, all died. This means (says Forsyth) that the human race was baptized into Christ's death. 'Before it could choose it received an infant baptism, so to speak, in Christ's death and resurrection.'[5] (How like his words are to those which Cullmann[6] was to use in his controversy with Barth in the 1940s: 'According to the New Testament, all men have in principle received baptism long ago, namely on Golgotha, at Good Friday and Easter. There the essential act of baptism was carried out, entirely without our co-operation, and even without our faith.')

Accordingly, the church's business is, with the Holy Spirit's help, to carry home what God in Christ has done, so that all men may have the chance to make it their own. Being made by the gospel – the gospel of a world already in principle redeemed – the church must mission to the world. As the trustee of this final revelation of God, the church, unless it betrays its trust, has no alternative but to engage in mission. Mission is its life's blood. 'It is not in our choice', Forsyth says, 'to spread the gospel or not. It is our death if we do not.'[7]

All this is a noble and true theology of the church and its calling. But in practice, as we all know, the church's task is made immensely difficult, especially in the mission-field, by our 'unhappy divisions'. This problem of the church's broken unity Forsyth had squarely faced in his time, and what he had to say is still worth pondering today by all who seek to break down the barriers that separate Christians from each other and blunt effective Christian witness to the pagan world.

First: proposals for reunion must never be based on mere expediency – the argument from efficiency. Any plan for reunion must have a theological basis, must proceed on the evangelical principle, namely that the church is one because it has one Redeemer who can only have one body. To found on evangelical principle instead of apparent efficiency (he said concerning plans for reunion) is vital in a religion of revelation, such as Christianity is.

Second: All questions of polity must be subservient to the gospel. No form of ecclesiastical constitution is sacrosanct – our modern re-reading of the New Testament is fatal both to monarchical episcopacy and to granular independency. ('I could do my work under a bishop, and feel honoured under the episcopate of many,' he said, 'but part of my work would be to preach that in the first century he did not exist.'[8]) Episcopacy is therefore optional, and the theory of apostolic succession, on which some base it, is untenable. The true apostolic succession is the evangelical – the succession of those who experience and proclaim the historic evangel of God's grace to sinners in Christ.

Third: 'The divisions of the churches can only be dealt with by federation; they are incurable along the line of absorption into one imperial church, or by the erasure of frontiers in an abstract and mystic fraternity.'[9] What we should aim at is a federation of honoured equals, a United States of the Church.

In any case the day of sectarianism is over. 'What victory can await a religion whose regiments have on them the curse of the clans and go each his own way with pride, following a chief but losing a Head?'[10] The task before Christendom today is to turn the splendid *ecclēsia* poetry of Paul in Ephesians into living fact.

One final question: What, in Forsyth's view, should be the church's strategy in its approach to the great secular society in which it has to live its life? This is a question which we shall have to take up more fully in the next chapter, when we discuss the church's role as the moral guide to society. Here we are simply concerned with Forsyth's view of the *modus operandi* which the church should adopt.

Should it be the method of 'inner mission' – preaching the gospel, celebrating the sacraments and engaging in philanthropy? No, this is too neutral. We churchmen have a duty to 'apply our holy faith to public conduct'.

Should the church then embark on a campaign of direct political action – a 'Party for Christ' perhaps? No, again: for the obvious reason that most churchmen do not have the necessary economic and political knowledge for such an enterprise. Yet, this said, Forsyth makes it clear that he will have no truck with those 'ethical vulgarians' who resent all Christian intrusion into public affairs and tell the clergy to mind their own business. The economic question, for example, so far from being a mere stomach question, is a moral and public one. There must ever be Christian concern to translate the gospel by which we live into social ethics which will match the needs of the time.

Has the church a right and duty to intervene in the great crisis of history and declare the will of God, as it sees it, without fear or favour? Yes, says Forsyth, who had himself in his younger days so intervened. None the less it was his considered judgment that the church's normal and wisest approach to the economic, social and political problems of the day was by way of education and influence rather than by direct intervention. Who are best fitted to do this work? Not, he thought, the clergy who have not the necessary specialized knowledge or experience for the task. But among the ranks of the laity there are men who have. It is their special expertise, informed by deep Christian principle, which is required. Mere piety without social sagacity will not do. 'We want an ethic of information both as to the cross and to the world. We must fully know our own gospel, the historic situation and business facts and methods.'[11] If we are to enter politics, we must enter them as practical men. Therefore one of the church's tasks should be to produce churchmen not only well grounded in the gospel, but from their knowledge of the world of commerce and politics,

86

fitted and ready to express the Christian viewpoint and play their part in advancing what should be the church's aim, the ethical conversion of an egoistic society.

How did Forsyth view the sacraments? Here too, as might be expected, he was a high churchman. He regarded them not as subsidiary extras, mere *parerga*, but as precious seals of God's saving grace in Christ and the cross. 'Sacraments, not socialities,' he wrote,[12] 'make the centre of our church life and social unity. Therefore make much of them.' As he cordially disapproved of baptism being administered in the home, so he disliked Zwinglian views of the Lord's supper. 'How.' he protested, 'can we have a memorial of One who is still alive, still our life?'

Consider his general doctrine of the sacraments. There is, he said, but one sacrament, that of the word, or gospel of God's grace in Christ, but it can be conveyed either by preaching or by sacrament (as we use the word) just as the Bible, properly used, becomes, by the Holy Spirit's action, 'the sacramental book'.

'The sacraments', he explained,[13] 'are the acted Word, variants of the preached Word. They are signs but more than signs. They are the Word itself, visible, as in true preaching the Word is audible. But in either case it is an act. It is Christ, in a real presence, giving us anew his redemption.' Acts of Christ really present by the Holy Spirit's power in the church – this is his doctrine, and it is a high one.

In what sense are the sacraments 'means of grace'? Not in the Roman way. At the idea of infused grace – 'spiritual inoculation' he called it – his gorge rose: the sacraments were mercy, not magic. Yet he insisted that they derive their virtue from an *opus operatum* – the act of the cross 'already accomplished and here (in the sacrament) delivered to our address', as he so vividly phrased it. They are not mere memorials or even symbols in the modern aesthetic sense. They are *energetic* symbols, symbols which contain and convey the significate, the

87

thing signified, by the work of the Spirit. They are 'Christ's love-tokens to his Body the Church' which convey Christ himself to the church because they deepen and enrich the saving personal relation between the Redeemer and the redeemed. And it is the church's duty to keep these 'love-tokens' bright not merely by care but by frequent use.

Now let us study his views of the two sacraments in more detail. The first point about baptism is that it is pre-eminently a sacrament of the church. This is why it should always be administered in face of the congregation and not (as was then often the practice) at home. In baptism the person baptized is stamped as God's property in a public way. Baptism beautifully symbolizes the prevenient grace of God, said Forsyth, using a homely illustration to enforce his point.[14]

A child's grandmother sometimes makes him the present of a christening mug which he uses as soon as he is big enough to sit at table with his elders. But a day comes when the child will ask who gave him the mug. He is told that it was his grandmother who loved him as a little child. 'Where is she?' 'She is dead.' 'And she loved me before I could speak – as soon as I was born?' 'Yes.' So (says Forsyth) love comes home to the child as a beautiful thing, an unseen, mysterious thing, a thing that was about his very beginning, and yet a thing that goes with him every day. This is a parable. The gift of the mug is baptism. It is a sign and seal of the prevenient grace of God, of the holy love that died to redeem us.

Baptism is a sacrament of the new life – of regeneration, but in a moral, not a magical, way. The church should use both forms of it – infant and adult – as is regularly done in the mission-field; for despite the lack of evidence for infant baptism in the New Testament (where what we have is the *praxis* of a missionary church), baptism *unto* faith has as good a right in the principle of the gospel, where grace precedes faith, as baptism *upon* faith.

Baptism means incorporation into the body of Christ where the Holy Spirit dwells and works, even if we cannot confine the operation of the Spirit to the limits of the church. It conveys

88

grace; but the conveyance, which is through the act and not the element (water), is more to the worshipping church than to the individual subject – unless of course he is able to take a conscious part in the worship. Hence in the case of an infant its effect is not immediate but *prospective*, since the blessing may only come years later when he realizes what Christ has done for him on the cross and of his own free will 'takes up' his membership. Baptized children are therefore members *in petto* – in reserve. At confirmation, which realizes the gift, they take up their church membership in strong earnest. Why not then delay baptism till years of discretion have come? To this Forsyth answers:[15] 'In Christ we are foredoomed to faith. Why not so commit the child in baptism, and cast God's mantle of grace over him?' But he also adds that baptism should never be given where there is no prospect of Christian upbringing. Thus, if baptism is a *door* – the appointed door of entrance into the church of Christ, the decisive setting of the individual within the body of Christ – and a *sign* of the love that died on Calvary to redeem us – it is also a *promise*, a promise by the parents that they will bring up their children in the Christian way, a promise also by the 'full members' of the church that they will do all they can to help it grow up 'in the nurture and discipline of the Lord'.

We turn now to the other sacrament, the Lord's supper or eucharist. Here we find Forsyth's treatment deeply satisfying because it seems to us so faithful to what the New Testament has to say about the last supper and the Lord's supper. Let anyone compare Forsyth's pages with the classical modern treatment of the subject, Jeremias's *Eucharistic Words of Jesus*, and he will note how at point after point they closely agree. (We do not mean that Forsyth goes into details about textual problems or argues at length that the last supper must have been a Passover, as Jeremias does. It is in their basic understanding of the meaning of the supper and the grace which it mediates that they substantially agree.)

Forsyth starts from the symbolic acts of the Old Testament prophets. Christ's actions in the upper room are of the same kind. They are energetic symbols. And the Lord's supper today is an act of the church created by an eternal act – the cross – which made and makes the church. These energetic symbols, whose meaning is not in the elements but in the action, convey the significate – the virtue of Christ's finished offering. It is Christ giving over to men the sacrifice he made once for all, for their redeeming, to God. (So Jeremias writes of the last supper: 'This is Jesus' last and greatest gift . . . A greater gift than a share in the redeeming power of his death Jesus could not give.')[16]

Go back (says Forsyth) to the upper room. It was a real act, the cross, that had to be symbolized; therefore a real act symbolized and conveyed it. The symbol lies in the breaking of the bread, not in the bread itself, and in the outpouring of the wine, not the wine itself. And in that energetic double symbol, corresponding to double parables in the gospels, Christ was making over the atonement in advance to the twelve as the nucleus of the new people of God which would arise in and through his death and resurrection.

The rite has three acts – breaking, giving and eating – which together make up the entire action in which Christ consigned to the Church the offering which he was making to God. 'This rite', says Jesus in effect, 'represents that the death I am dying is for you. Your act of eating represents the way in which you must assimilate me crucified and given to God. In this way you appropriate the benefits of my atoning death.' Clearly the disciples understood Christ to be setting up a closer communion with himself, uniting them in a 'new covenant'. The new thing was not the mere fraternity but its cohesion in his ever-present lordship through the cross.

So today, through the work of the Holy Spirit, a living and present Christ continues that gift for our response in a church's faith. 'It is not that the finished sacrifice is offered to God afresh,' says Forsyth,[17] 'even by Christ, still less by a priest; but the sacrifice made once for all functions afresh.' And what the confessors of Christ get in the sacrament is forgiveness rather than food, not spiritual medicine but moral mercy, as through the Holy Spirit's power the gospel of God's redeeming love in the cross reverberates for their upbuilding and growth in grace.

NOTES

1. Quoted by Anders Nygren in *Christ and His Church*, SPCK 1957.
2. *C. and S.*, p. 57.
3. *Ibid.*
4. See *RON*, chapter 3.
5. *RON*, p. 36.
6. *Baptism in the New Testament*, SCM Press 1950, p. 23.
7. *RON*, p. 54.
8. *C. and S.*, p. 42.
9. *CEW*, p. 3.
10. *C. and S.*, p. 6.
11. *CGS*, p. 49.
12. *C. and S.*, p. 229.
13. *Ibid*, p. 165.
14. *Ibid*, p. 162.
15. *Ibid*, p. 206.
16. *The Eucharistic Words of Jesus*, SCM Press 1966, p. 236.
17. *C. and S.*, p. 256.

8

Christian Ethic

Carlyle somewhere tells the story of Lord Rea who, when things looked very black, said to Sir David Ramsay, 'Well, God mend all!' 'Nay, by God, Donald,' replied Sir David, 'we must help him to mend it.' Theologians who stress the seriousness of sin and magnify God's grace have sometimes been credited with a 'God-mend-all' frame of mind and accused of ethical quietism. No such charge could be laid at Forsyth's door. As his theology had been hammered out not in some cloistered academe but in the hurly-burly of ministering to working people in great cities, so he had no patience with a Christian faith which did not attest itself in moral action and carry clear social implications. In one place he talks of the 'ethical vulgarism' of those who would divorce religion from politics and bid Christians be silent on the social questions of the day. Christian love, he said, must give up 'cooing' and get down to business. Nor was he himself slow to speak out on the big moral, social and political issues of his time. How then did he interpret the Christian ethic and the role the church ought to play in society?

1. *The Source of Christian Morals*

When Forsyth discusses the Christian ethic he generally makes three main points.

1. The first is that *ultimately there are no ethics but theological*.[1] What did he mean? Are there no such things as 'natural ethics'?

For the convenience of discussion we may distinguish between theological and natural ethics. But morals are merely academic which fail to deal with that most formidable and intractable fact of all – human sin and guilt. We must take man in his actual historical situation; and when we do this, the so-called 'natural conscience' does not exist, it is a mere abstraction. What actually exists is the historical product, the sinful conscience. This is the lesson which human solidarity and heredity teach us, and this is the point where the humanist 'morals without religion' break down. It is told of Frederick the Great that, as he listened to a preacher descanting eloquently on the natural goodness of man, he growled out, 'He doesn't know the perishing human race.' So Forsyth faulted humanist ethics for their failure to reckon with 'the great human soul lamed and doomed with the malady of sin'.

2. We are ready now for Forsyth's second and capital point – *the cross is the centre and source of Christian ethics*.[2] Ask a representative group of Christians today what should be the basis for a proper Christian ethic, and the odds are they would answer: 'The moral teaching of Jesus – especially the precepts of the Sermon on the Mount.' Not so, said Forsyth, the cross and not the sermon is the source of Christian morals.

Forsyth's reply is not so startling to us nowadays who have learned from C. H. Dodd and others what was the true relation between religion and ethics in the early church. The first and distinctive thing in the apostles' message was the *kērygma* – the declaration of God's gracious saving action in the cross and resurrection. Only after this proclamation, and in its context, came the *didachē*, the pattern of Christian living expected of those who by accepting the apostolic gospel had become members of the new people of God, the church of Christ.

In Forsyth's day, however, his rootage of the Christian ethic in the grace of the cross, instead of in the precepts of the sermon must have seemed not only wrong but wrong-headed. How did he defend this cross-centred concept of Christian morals?

It is quite misguided and unrealistic, he said,[3] to take our stand on Christ's precepts and seek to apply them directly to our problems today, for the simple and obvious reason that almost two thousand years have come and gone and the world

93

has changed so vastly in the interval. To take two examples only: would Christ today have said what he said to his disciples in Galilee – tell us to give to everyone who asks and forbid us to keep a balance in the bank?

No, this 'preceptual' approach to Christian ethics tends to turn Christ into a legislator, a second and greater Moses, and to set up a new Judaism. The mistake is to imagine that the kingdom of God was set up in the precepts of the sermon when in fact it was set up in the cross on the hill and its tremendous sequel. Indeed to suppose that Christ's action on the world is 'preceptual' and the New Testament a kind of Christian code, is to 'fall from grace with Galatian levity'. For precepts, which are local and sometimes temporary, have a way of becoming outdated as well as open to casuistry. Further, we forget that the apostles themselves – witness the epistles – generally appeal to the spirit and temper of Christ rather than to his precepts. They freely prescribe Christian duties from the new mind which has been produced by grace.

In a sentence, the source of Christian ethic is, like that of worship, not the Sermon on the Mount but the moral inwardness and creativeness of the cross which contains, along with the power, the principle meant to solve our moral problems, now as then.

3. This brings us to Forsyth's third point. *Real forgiveness such as the penitent sinner receives at the cross, is in the same act quickening and regenerating.*[4] True faith *is* really salvation, and not merely something rewarded with salvation. To be forgiven much (like the woman who was a sinner, as described in Luke 7) is to love much, which is to live much and to live anew. Christians are those who live by such saving faith and work through love, which is the rose-bloom on their faith. In other words, Christian goodness is 'grace goodness' – our spontaneous reaction, in Chritian living, to God's mercy towards us in the cross of Christ where he not only sets us in right relations with himself but unleashes in us a new power impelling us in gratitude to deeds of Christian love and service. For the forgiving grace of God is the mightiest and most

permanent power in the moral world. Knowing ourselves forgiven by God for Christ's sake, we are moved to forgive others. Our good works are really an expression of gratitude to the God who on the cross has not only borne our sins but by the power of his grace created in us a principle of new life. So, with the Spirit's help, we are called to become what we potentially are – new men and women in Christ.

Thus Forsyth understands the regenerative power of divine forgiveness. It is good apostolic doctrine and in accord with Erskine of Linlathen's *dictum*: 'In the New Testament religion is grace and ethics is gratitude.'[5] Let us sum up this section in Forsyth's own amended version of Augustine's saying: 'Love (as the holy and atoning cross creates love) and do what you will. That is Christian ethic.'[6]

2. *The Problem of Christian Vocation*

A Christianity which merely changes the individual and does nothing to change society is, said Forsyth, quite inadequate. There must be social as well as individual change. What then has Forsyth to say about the Christian social ethic and the church's role (to use his own phrase) as 'the moral guide of society'?

Before we summarize his views, we must hear him on a point[7] obvious enough yet often forgotten by Christian preachers today when they tell their congregations to glorify God in their daily lives and perhaps quote George Herbert:

> Teach me, my God and King,
> In all things thee to see,
> And what I do in anything
> To do it as for thee.

It is the whole problem of Christian vocation in the modern world.

At the Reformation, with monasticism in his mind's eye, Luther rightly declared that Christians could serve God as truly in their daily work as in their Sunday worship. This was a great step forward. But why does this Protestant conception of

95

Christian vocation sound much less convincing today? Because we live in a quite different world from Luther's. In the sixteenth century most people belonged to some church; nowadays perhaps a majority do not. Moreover, we have passed from closed areas of trade (such as Luther knew) to illimitable world-trade – from the world of monasticism to the world of economics and high finance.

Thus the whole issue of Christian vocation has become much more difficult. How is a Christian business man today to serve God in his daily work when 'the rat race' of commercial competition drives him to make money as best he can in order to provide for his family, illness and old age? Is money-making in itself a divine vocation? Or take the editor who is forced to put his paper's circulation before his education of the public, to give the public what they like, not what they need. How can a Christian journalist fulfil his vocation if circumstances compel him in what he writes to pander to 'the permissive society' of the day? Or how can an honest inn-keeper fulfil his Christian vocation when, willy-nilly, he is identified with 'the drink interest' which produces alcoholics and indirectly causes much of the crime and violence in our society? Shall we tell him to leave his job and go out in faith like Abraham, not knowing where he goes? If we could assure him of another source of livelihood, all might be well. But, if we cannot, what is to happen to his wife and family?

Nor is this the whole of the Christian worker's problem. When Luther spelt out the Christian doctrine of vocation, there was no modern division of labour. A Christian artisan could put his whole moral self into the article he began and finished. Now he is but a cog in a great machine – or one human stage in a long conveyor-belt – turning out only a tiny fragment of the finished article, as he is condemned to a life of drudging and joyless monotony. How can a Christian man like this serve God in his daily work as Luther counselled him to do?

The long and the short of it is that Christian ethics cannot now rest content with calling on such people to glorify God in their station. We of the Christian church must seek to promote such a re-organization of industry as will give the worker freedom to live as a man should, find joy in his work, be able to maintain his family, and become a responsible partner, to some degree, in that industry of which he is a part. In short, if *agapē* remains the master-key to Christian morals, it must express itself in Christian action which is more principle than sentiment.

We have dwelt at some length on one specific problem of Christian social ethics, in order to show how modern and down-to-earth this so-called 'neo-orthodox' theologian can be.

3. *The Church as the Moral Guide of Society*

The finest account of Forsyth's views on the ethical role of the church in our modern society is contained in the long address he gave, as chairman of the Congregational Union, under the title of 'A Holy Church the Moral Guide of Society'. It has recently been reprinted as the first part of a volume entitled *The Church, the Gospel and Society*. To this the reader is referred. Nothing could better show how much hard thinking Forsyth had devoted to the problem of how the church should seek to apply its faith to the social and economic disorder and disease of our day. All we can attempt here is a summary of what he has to say.

The great problem before civilization, he begins, is the moral one. The life of society contains two main elements, the economic and the moral; but these two are basically one, which is ethical. Therefore the church has a right to intrude into the economic and political issues of the day and 'apply holy faith to public conduct'. And what we need is a Christian moral doctrine of society.

We live in a time characterized by the conflict between capitalism and socialism. Capitalism, he says, was a necessary stage in the providential conduct of the world; but if it brought with it blessings, it brought also banes – above all, the curse of immense private wealth in non-moral hands, with the result that the weak and the poor too often went to the wall. The rise of Socialism was an inevitable and just protest against unfettered capitalism; but we must not suppose that it contains the

Christian social ethic which we need, because it is based on a morality of natural rights and tends to ignore the spiritual principle which is the only Christian basis of brotherhood.

The church's aim should be the ethical conversion of society by the application of Christian principles to the burning social and economic issues of the time. The real conflict is not between capitalism and labour, but between the egoism at the heart of our society and the gospel which has alone the cure for it – the regeneration of the sinful men who make up society. As the moral guide of society, the church's aim should be to translate her holy gospel into large, social ethics relevant to the time. If the church is to be effective in this task, she will need much more than mere piety. ('One of the greatest moral dangers', says Forysth[8] 'is a truly pious man with a conventional morality in the midst of a great crisis.') She will need to turn out Christian experts in economic affairs, preferably laymen; for ministers, by reason of the nature of their calling, are generally ill equipped to handle such issues.

The church's record in philanthropy has been a splendid one; but philanthropy by itself is no longer enough. The church's need is of men able to probe the root-cause in the sickness of our modern society – men who know the economic situation as well as the Old Testament prophets did theirs in their day – and can produce practical policies for redeeming society from its egoism, ensuring that social justice is really done in the land, and fit to pressurize governments in great national and international crises. (In government, said Forsyth, we need the statesmanship of men who are not only Christians but have a grasp of Christianity as well as sympathy with it.)

In short, the church (and Forsyth apologizes for the metaphor) should be a 'factory' for turning out men able to cope with the problem of adjusting 'gold and the gospel, faith and finance, love and egoism'. He has no illusions about the difficulty of the church's task in its attempt to convert our society and establish a social order based on the Christian principle of brotherhood. On the other hand, he is no less convinced that the church has in its holy gospel the only spiritual power which can regenerate society. 'Our true capital', he says,[9] 'is our moral capital. Even in the passing world the true capital is not money, but ideas, conscience, justice. All the resources of nature were no wealth without men, without mind. Wealth means value to moral beings. So in the church: its true capital is neither its traditions, nor its institutions, neither its tithes, nor even its creeds. It is its holy faith and love and the sagacity of both for the social soul.' The church's main task is not to solve the social problem but 'to provide the men, the principles, and the public it can.' Therefore the church must provide authoritative voices who can speak on her behalf out of the fullness of their holy faith, to the strength, and not the weakness, of the busy world. Such men should be experts on the moral problems created by the economic life. Let the church discover such men, and she will be well on the way to fulfilling her role of being a moral guide to society.

To sum up Forsyth's whole thinking on the Christian ethic. The church, he held, had an ethic not only for the individual but for society and the world beyond the confines of the church, the world in which capitalists and socialists join issue with each other, the world which is ever troubled by the supreme issue of peace or war. The source of that ethic lay in the cross. We may sum up the Christian ethic as love; but, as the cross shows, love, if it is to be truly Christian, can never be severed from righteousness which is, as Forsyth said, 'applied holiness'. In fact the public form of love is righteousness. Once grasp this point, and the Christian attitude to the wider issues, social, economic, political and international, becomes clear. In the realm of industrial relations Christian love will take the form of a demand for social justice and an insistence that if the present industrial order stifles the Christian life and rides roughshod over Christian values, the order must be changed. So too in the great issue of peace and war. If the cross is what it is (said Forsyth in *The Christian Ethic in War*) – God's judgment in Christ on human sin – then the men who identify themselves with Christ, i.e. the church, have the right to judge sin on a national and international scale (e.g. Germany's in the First

99

World War) and to use force in the name of the kingdom of God. (We can only speculate about what his opinion would have been if he had lived in an age menaced by the dread fear of nuclear holocaust.)

In short, for Forsyth Christian ethics are grounded in the gospel of grace. They are concerned not only with the individual but with society and with nations. But Christianity is not bound up with any particular political or social system; it must reserve the right to criticize all or any in the light of Christian principle; and since the gospel must speak with relevance and power to every such issue, the church's strategy must be an ever growing and changing thing. So he prayed for the church:

We beseech thee, O Lord, for thy church throughout the world. May it grow in the faith of the cross and the power of the resurrection. Keep it in thy eternal unity, in great humility, in godly fear, and in thine own pure and peaceable wisdom so easy to be entreated. Make it swift and mighty in the cause of the Kingdom of God. Cover, stablish and enlighten it, that it may see through all that darkens the time, and move it in the shadow of thy wing, with faith, obedience and sober power.'[10]

NOTES

1. *POA*, pp. 403ff. Cf. *TGAA*, pp. 172f.
2. *PPMM*, pp. 325f. Cf. *C. and S.*, p. 32.
3. *CGS*, pp. 16f.
4. *C. and S.*, p. 186. Cf. *JOG*, p. 220.
5. W. Hanna (ed.), *Letters of Thomas Erskine*, Edinburgh 1877, I, p. 16.
6. *CEW*, p. 137.
7. *CGS*, pp. 49–55.
8. *British Weekly*, 12 May 1904.
9. *CGS*, p. 64.
10. *Intercessory Services for aid in Public Worship*, J. Heywood (Manchester) 1896, p. 18.

9

Christian Theodicy

'Theodicy' (from the Greek *theos* 'God' and *dikē* 'justice') describes that part of theology concerned to defend the goodness and omnipotence of God against objections arising from the existence of evil in the world. It was this problem which the outbreak of the First World War posed, in letters of blood and fire for Forsyth's generation, and evoked from him what some have thought his most powerful book, *The Justification of God*. Now inevitably a little 'dated', it reveals none the less abiding insights into our human situation under God, and it ends with a Christian solution to the riddle of history which finds its key in the cross. A God (he argues) who can deal in mercy with the tragedy of man's sin and guilt, as God has done in the cross of his Son, has fully in hand, at long last, the misery and mystery of man's fate.

But this is to anticipate. At the outset, the reader should be warned that the book's twelve chapters do not make easy reading. Indeed, Forsyth invites any, if they so wish, to 'skip' chapter 3 (on 'metaphysics and redemption') because only those interested will make anything of it. This chapter aside, the book advances 'theologically but not systematically' because the writer has a way of pausing to indict the church, now for its shallow or its ossified version of the faith, now for its failure to contain and control the forces of international strife.

Yet, dated and difficult though it is, the book contains some of Forsyth's greatest passages, and its main burden is as relevant now as it was in 1917. At the beginning of the Second World War David S. Cairns declared: 'When your foot is on the rock, you can exult even in the whirlpool.' *The Justification of God* can set a Christian's feet on the rock – the Rock of Ages – and inspire in him the certitude that the long travail of history has a divine meaning and goal.

I

To help the ordinary reader understand the book as a whole we propose to start with a brief summary, later to be expanded. World calamity, says Forsyth in his 'overture', raises acutely the problem of theodicy. The failure of popular Christianity to cope with world tragedy is the theme of the first chapter. With chapter 2 we pass to the question, Has the world a divine goal, and if so, where are we to look for a clue to it? The burden of chapter 3 is that we have no real evidence that the moral order of the world contains within it a self-healing power to restore the breach made in it by awful crises of evil like world-wars. What is needed to heal the race's spiritual wound, declares chapter 4, is a redemptive act of the holy God in history. And, says chapter 5, what God has given us is not a scheme of rational optimism promising progress spreading to the perfect day but an effected redemption assuring faith that the world has a divine goal. In chapter 6 reasons are given for the church's sorry failure to prevent strife among the nations.

With chapter 7 Forsyth begins to rise to the height of his argument. There is no theodicy for the world except in a proper theology of the cross. God must justify himself, and this he has done in Christ crucified. But will not the philosophers' attempts at theodicy meet our need is the question raised in chapter 8. No, because when faced with the stark realities of evil on a great scale, they either minimize them or explain them away. With chapter 9 we come to the cruciality of the cross for human destiny. If the holy God did not spare his own Son, i.e. his own self, his holiness is finally secured for the whole race, and we may be sure that no tragedy in history is outside his control or impossible for his purpose. Our hope of a divine destiny for the world rests on what God has already done for us, once for all, in Christ. He is the theodicy of God, and the justifier both of God and the ungodly. Chapters 10 and 11 discuss God's saving judgment. Chapter 12, which forms the 'coda' to his opening 'overture' and is entitled 'the conquest of time by eternity', sums up the whole argument and brings in eternity to redress the injustices of time. Christ crucified and risen is the final answer to the riddle of life. In the cross and resurrection God in Christ triumphed over all evil, and by union with him we are beneficiaries in that conquest of his which secured the world's future, as it assures the Christian that the spinal cord of history is redemption, and that the Holy One must finally vanquish all evil, and in heaven make all earth's mysteries plain.

II

We may now go back to the beginning and spell out the argument in some detail. The catastrophe of a world war faces us anew with the old dilemma (says Forsyth): 'If God has power to stop these things, and he does not, he is not good. If he is good, and does not, he is not omnipotent.' Before plunging *in medias res*, he lets fall a hint that his theodicy will find its key to the riddle of history in Christ and his cross. Then he turns to 'the fundamental heresy of the day', humanism, now deeply embedded in Christianity itself. Man-centred and not God-centred, our popular Christianity is more anxious to have God on its side than to be on God's. It is like the small boy who said, 'I will pray to God all this week for an engine, and if he does not give it to me, I will worship idols.' Having ceased to 'bother about sin', we find the onset of calamity inexplicable. So 'God enters the pulpit and preaches in his own way by deeds, and his sermons are long and taxing, and they spoil the dinner.'[1]

How much wickeder the world is than our dear and dainty piety had supposed! Now we begin to see the need of a vaster Christ and a diviner salvation. 'None but a supramundane Christ can cope with such evil as comes home to us now. And what we now realize of evil is but a fraction of what the holy eye has seen, his heart borne, and his redemption engaged since history began.'[2] God's account of himself and his ways with men is in the New Testament Christ, or it is nowhere. There is but one theodicy – one justification of God and his ways in this world – and it is apostolic and evangelical (ch. 1).

Man's malaise diagnosed, Forsyth turns to the question, Has the world a divine *telos* or goal – both for the soul and for the race? Creation means life, movement, evolution. But what is its drift and to what end, if any, is it moving? We cannot trace it in the course and curve of history which so often looks like 'one darned thing after another'. Has history any revelationary point, one historic spot where 'the world comes to a head and God comes to his own'? Christianity says that it has. There is one point where time is no longer and passes into eternity. That point is Christ. The final theodicy is to be found not in any philosopher's system but in the redemption wrought by God in Christ. 'To know Christ's God, as apostles expound his revelation, is to know the long dominants of order and purpose in nature and history.'[3] Already it is becoming clear that the diamond pivot on which Forsyth's theodicy will turn is the cross and God's seal on it in the resurrection (ch. 2).

Before developing his theodicy further, Forsyth raises the question, Does the doctrine of evolution encourage us to hold that there is in the moral order of the world a self-recuperative process – a *vis medicatrix* like that in physical organisms – which may be trusted to heal the dreadful breach in it created by this crisis of evil, and recreate humanity? Alas, there is no real evidence for it. Physical analogies are not enough, for all are limited. There comes a point when the power of physical self-repair ceases – in death. A tendency to self-recuperation we *may* find in the process of nature apart from redemption, but not a power, a certainty, a finality. No merely evolutionary process can deal justly with the race's moral tragedy or heal its deep-seated wound. What is needed is a holy redemptive act of God in history – an act which involves a second creation, a new humanity (ch. 3).

What do we mean by redemption? What the Absolute is to the philosopher, the Holy is to the theologian. Both face the question, Will the Ultimate Power finally prevail over all the world's chaos and woe? Your philosopher answers in terms of a pantheistic mysticism and dreams of 'one God, one law, one element'. Your theologian answers in terms of a personalist creation, and a goal of God's appointing reached not by process but by crisis, not by growth but by rescue. Between them we must choose. Christianity stresses crisis rather than order. For it, redemption means an active revelation of the Holy One, and the final issue the return of humanity to God. Those who began as his natural creatures are to end as his redeemed sons. The Christian hope is of a moral realm of persons made perfect on a universal and eternal scale by the grace of a holy God. To humanity, its faith and hope almost eclipsed by world catastrophe, the infinite and most merciful Majesty yet says, 'Fear not, little flock, it is your Father's good pleasure to *give* you the Kingdom' (ch. 4).

'Salvation theological, not systematic' is how Forsyth describes the next step in his argument. What God has given us (he means) is not a scheme of rational optimism, pledging us progress gradually spreading to the perfect day, but the promise of final victory based on a victory already won on the cross. If he has not offered us a programme of happy things, in Christ and the atonement he has given us love, and faith, with himself to trust and obey. If he has not provided us with a pattern of his operations, he has forgiven a guilty race in the cross by a saving act which has now created the world. Civilization may collapse but the divine sovereignty set up in the cross remains invincible, and no storm of history can sweep away the soul that is anchored on the gospel of that atoning deed which established God's eternal moral kingdom. We are more than conquerors through him who loved us and gave himself for us (ch. 5). (In the rest of the chapter Forsyth criticizes the Free Churches for trivializing the gospel, and Anglicanism for intellectualizing it. Both lack the moral note which has been the glory of Puritanism. With so much non-moral religion about in a world sunk in materialism, is it any wonder, he asks, that the one Judge of the earth now does right?)

The church, alas, seems unable to provide men with a

theodicy equal in power to the tragedy which now engulfs the world. Here it is concerned with the question of how to restrain the forces of international strife after the war. This is 'trying to meet the Atlantic with a mop'. Churchmen have totally misgauged the civilization which carried this war in its womb. What the church ought to be doing is to recapture the historic gospel which alone can match man's deepest need. The present judgment is on a godless civilization of which we are a part, and our man-centred religion is much to blame for it. 'The anomaly is not that a God of love should permit such things as we see. In the egoist condition of our civilization, and with a God of holy love over all, the scandal would have been if such judgments had not come'[4] (ch. 6).

Half way through his book Forsyth now begins to rise to the height of his great argument. The last demand of the soul is that God should vindicate his ways to men. The Christian reply is that he has – in Christ. In the cross the Holy One has been seen 'putting things right'. There the whole issue of warring history is condemned. There good and evil met for good and all. 'There is no theodicy for the world', he says, 'except in a theology of the cross.'[5] God must justify himself, and he did so in the cross of his Son. To redeem creation was a harder thing than to create it. All the energy of a perverse world which God had trusted with freedom pulled on the knot which Christ had to undo. And its undoing by God in Christ's cross gives us the clue to all God's dealings with the world. There God in Christ overcame the world, hallowed his own name, and created it anew in the Spirit. (If this was not the world-work God gave Christ to do, Christ was a megalomaniac, for he believed it was, and he infected the apostles with his belief.)

Do not misunderstand the present cataclysm and God's judgment now upon us, comments Forsyth. It is but the condensation of what has been going on for a very long time. This flare has long been smouldering, and 'the dirty chimney had to be fired'. If only we had learned from the Old Testament prophets, we should have found it strange if judgment had *not* fallen on us. But the cross, which is the key to a Christian theodicy, so far from being merely a theological theme, is the supreme crisis of the moral world, a crisis far greater than any earthly war; and in it we see God dealing with the whole soul of the world in holy love (ch. 7).

Before developing this theme further, Forsyth pauses to consider how philosophy handles the grim facts of suffering and sin. Your philosopher, he says, regards the gulf between the holy and the sinful as more apparent than real, sees it as something which the onward march of progress will bridge and dispel. So he 'grafts the untoward on to the good' in a rational way. Either he uses the Buffer method, reducing the impact of the perverse fact on the general mass. Or, employing the Shunt method, he averts the collision by turning the grievance on to a loop line. So, for him, banes become disguised boons, aches 'growing pains', and evil but 'good in the making'. Alas, these ivory-tower reasonings cannot adequately explain a crisis when all hell seems let loose in the world. Such philosophic theodicies, he concludes, 'break in our hands when applied to the last anomalies of the soul'. The secret of the Lord is not with the philosopher but with the prophet – the prophet who understands aright the fact of Christ (ch. 8).

Now, at long last, we come to the very heart of the matter and the book's supreme chapter – 'the eternal cruciality of the Cross for human destiny'. 'The only theodicy', says[6] our author, 'is that which redeems and from the nettle perdition plucks the flower of salvation.' That happened in Christ's cross. There God in Christ so died that sin lost its chief servant, death, which now became the minister of life-eternal life. Now 'if the greatest act in the world, and the greatest crime, there became by the moral, the holy victory of the Son of God, the source not only of endless blessing to man but of perfect satisfaction and delight to holy God, then there is no crime, not even this war, that is outside his control or impossible for his purpose'.[7] God's wisdom none may be able to trace by human reason; but his act finds us. In the cross we learn the faith that 'things not willed by God are yet worked up by God' and, by a divine irony, 'man's greatest crime turns God's greatest boon.'[8]

In what God has done for the world, once for all, in Christ, we have our master-clue to the goal which God designs for it. More, it provides the Christian with ground for assurance in the present. Here the Holy Spirit enables us to realize 'the simultaneity of eternity in time'. 'If we look back, faith, by the Spirit, abolishes time, and finds the fontal Christ of long ago to be the fundamental power of today. He rose upon history in a remote age. and he rises now in history from its profoundest depths.'[9] Therefore 'faith's greatest conquest is to believe, on the strength of Christ's cross, that the world has been overcome, and that the nations which rage so furiously are still in the leash of the redeeming God'.

On God's *modus operandi* in vindicating his ways to men Christian faith must bear two things in mind: first, that God's method is one of election; second, that it is one of sorrow: 'the Captain of the elect was not spared the Cross'. On the first point: we have no right to prescribe a rational programme for the almighty wisdom and call on God to comply with it. In God's way to his goal, as the Bible shows, he remains absolutely free. Crisis, choice, judgment, sifting, election, conversion and new departure by new creation age after age are how God works; and from the non-elect in one age comes the elect for the next. But the second point is perhaps the one which troubles us more, and it is this: Why does suffering befall good and bad, elect and non-elect, alike?

To this question there is no rational answer but there is a *revealed* one – in the cross. The agony and devilry of war horrify us – though they but condense in a crisis what has long been accumulating – and we cry out at the cost. 'Do you stumble at the cost?' God says to us in the cross that

It has cost Me more than you . . . It cost Me my only Son to justify my name of righteousness and to realize the destiny of my creature in holy love. And all mankind is not so great and dear as He. Nor is its suffering the enormity in a moral world that his Cross is. I am no mere spectator of the course of things. I spared not my own Son. We carried the load that crushes you. It bowed him into the ground. On the third day he rose with a new creation in his hand and a regenerate world, and all things working together for good to love and the holy purpose in love. And what he did I did. How I did it? How I do it? This you know not how, and could not, but you shall know hereafter. There are things the Father must keep in his own hand. Be still and know that I am God whose mercy is as his majesty, and his omnipotence is chiefly in forgiving, and redeeming, and settling all souls in worship in the temple of a new heaven and earth full of holiness. In that day the anguish will be forgotten for joy that a New Humanity is born into the world.[10]

The whole passage is quintessential Forsyth. It presupposes his doctrine of the atonement – that of a holy Father self-atoned in his Son. It does not shrink from the idea of Patri-passianism – the doctrine that God suffers. It sees the final issue of the world's reconciliation, wrought in principle on the cross, in the vision of a great new humanity and a regenerated race. And it asserts that 'there is not room enough in this world for God's eschatology'.

What we needed to justify the ways of God with men in a world of evil was a revelation in action. It came in the cross. There the righteousness of God was not only dreamed but done – and done in a world not of suffering alone but still more of sin. In Christ's obedience even unto death we have the perfect satisfaction the Holy finds in the Holy. In this act Christ acted racially – he was the new humanity doing the one needful and rightful thing before God. (Since the satisfaction was made by the Son of God, it was made by God, for God could be atoned by no third party.) Therefore Christian faith can be sure that, 'whether in maelstrom or volcano', the world is God's and good must be the final goal of ill (ch. 9).

Before he sums up, Forsyth meditates in two chapters on the implications of his theodicy, and especially on God's judgments in history – those crises (and 'crisis' is Greek for 'judgment') or times of God's great sifting action among men and nations which show that the course of history has a moral fabric which man, *improbus homo*, defies at his peril.

First, God's judgment is *saving* judgment. We tend to regard 'grace' and 'judgment' as diametrical opposites. They are really two sides of the same divine coin. Because God is holy he must judge sin, but his purpose in so judging is to save. The cross, which is our key to history, was both judgment on sin and grace for the sinner in one great historic act. Second: judgment is a word with three tenses. It is a past event, a present process, and a future settlement. In principle, the last judgment was effected on the cross. There God in Christ judged and saved the world for good and all. Yet Schiller's saying 'world history is world judgment' has its truth. Even now in the crises of history God is judging and saving souls and civilizations, 'sifting out the hearts of men before his judgment seat'. These judgments of God in history are his practical theodicy, and need no apologia. In the cross we have the key to them; for the cross enacts on an eternal scale the moral principle which is subduing all history to itself. But, third, present judgment in history does not exclude the idea of a final judgment. 'There is a goal of history and a theodicy in the grand style and it is a last judgment (whatever form it takes) according to God's grace,' says Forsyth.[11] But, he adds, the cross was the last judgment unto salvation; and if we shall face it at the end, it is only because we now face it at bottom.

Two further points of capital importance Forsyth makes. First, the last judgment of the cross gives us an absolute point of vantage from which to view all other crises and read all history. 'History', he says[12] 'can only be understood by something which is final in history as well as beyond history.' Again, 'high history is not possible without the teleology which a final judgment supplies for all other crises'.[13] (Thirty years after Forsyth Donald Baillie[14] said the same thing. We cannot interpret history, he asserted, until we get an absolute point of vantage from which to view it, and this is to be found in Christ.) Why does the secular historian's empirical analysis of events disclose no discernible purpose running through history and intelligible in terms of its end? Because to him all events are *relative*, and he lacks *an absolute point of vantage* from which to survey them. It is precisely this, says Forsyth, which the

Christian has in Christ and his cross. The cross is the point of revelation which gives us in one act the ground of history and the goal of tomorrow, presents us in advance with the purpose and destiny of the world. 'The key to history is the historic Christ, above it and in command of it, and there is no other.'[15] More, the future can add nothing in principle to the great settlement between good and evil made at Calvary.

Second: if God's judgment in history often seems to delay, it is none the less sure. God moves in long orbits, out of sight and sound. Yet the almighty *Cunctator Maximus* is incessantly passing judgment on men – sometimes giving us our desires and shrivelling our souls, sometimes making of our pleasant vices instruments to scourge us. Slow God may seem to our earth-bound vision, but he always arrives. 'The world gets a long time to pay, but all the accounts are kept . . . Lest if anything were forgotten, there might be something unforgiven, unredeemed, unholy still.'[16] (chs. 10 and 11).

In his 'coda' Forsyth sums up his long argument and concludes. Life is a problem (he begins), a struggle and not a stroll. More, as Nietzsche, whose mind was unhinged by it, saw, it is a tragic tangle. Yet *pace* pessimists like Thomas Hardy, it has a solution. The answer is there, and it is God's gift in Christ. Not a philosophical solution, but a practical one. It comes not by thought but by faith – faith in the God and Father of Christ. The solution lies outside life in that eternal order which in Christ and his cross and resurrection has invaded time. At the cross God's judgment of the world is not only seen but done. (Were the cross a mere martyrdom, nothing would be solved.) Christ not only assures us of a divine issue to history but secures it. If all things are not yet put under righteousness, we see Christ now 'crowned with glory and honour'.

Now in his victory over evil Christ was no lone individual but the agent of the race. If he overcame the world, it was humanity that won; and by union with the Victor we are beneficiaries in his conquest. 'Christ crucified and risen is the final eternal answer to the riddle of life. One day when we sit in heavenly places in Christ, we shall see the tangle of life unroll and fall into shape . . . We shall see guilt destroyed; and with that, death, wrong, darkness and grief.'[17] For over every tragedy of earth stands the eternal reconciliation God made in Christ. True, the end is not yet – the campaign between good and evil still drags on; but 'the evil world will not win at last because it failed to win the only time it ever could. It is a vanquished world in which men play their devilries. Christ has overcome it'.[18] (ch. 12).

Such is Forsyth's theodicy. Thus characteristically he finds in the atoning cross the light needed to illumine the dark scroll of history. His solution is nothing if not fully Christian; indeed he says there is no other.

Centuries before the man of Uz had wrestled with the problem of the Almighty's dealings with men as personalized in his own tragedy. Now in Christ, Forsyth says, God has given his answer to Job's demand that he should vindicate his ways with men. His answer is in a person who is in history yet above it. The answer is not a mere revelation; it is a redemptive act and a moral victory which has in principle recovered the race. The Vindicator has stood on the earth. He is Christ crucified, risen and regnant, the eternal Son of God. In his work the dread knot created by God's holiness and man's sin and drawn into a tight 'snarl' by mankind's misuse of its God-given freedom, has been undone. And God's undoing of it in his Son's cross provides the key to all his dealings with men, as it gives us his master-clue to his final destiny for the world and the race – a moral sovereignty without end, a recreated humanity, and a consummation of all things in the eternal kingdom of God.

NOTES

1. *JOG*, p. 28.
2. *Ibid*, p. 32.
3. *Ibid*, p. 58.
4. *Ibid*, p. 119.

5. *Ibid*, p. 122.
6. *Ibid*, p. 156.
7. *Ibid*, p. 151.
8. *Ibid*, p. 154.
9. *Ibid*, pp. 157f.
10. *Ibid*, pp. 164f.
11. *Ibid*, p. 181.
12. *Ibid*, p. 217.
13. *Ibid*, p. 190.
14. *God was in Christ*, Charles Scribner's 1948, p. 73.
15. *JOG*, p. 218.
16. *Ibid*, p. 207.
17. *Ibid*, p. 221.
18. *Ibid*, p. 223.

This Life and the Next

When the American poet and naturalist, Henry Thoreau, lay dying, his friend Parker Pillsbury, who sat by his bed-side, leaned over, took him by the hand, and said, 'Henry, you are so near to the border now. Can you see anything on the other side?' 'One world at a time,' replied the dying man, 'one world at a time, Parker.'

Such a reply on the lips of Forsyth is unthinkable. Eternity for him did not simply lie at the end of time, neither was it something only to be experienced after death. He could not agree that Thoreau's two worlds were so unrelated to each other, or that our Christian experience in this life had nothing to teach us about:

> The undiscovered country from whose bourn
> No traveller returns.

When in 1918 he wrote his last book – a slim volume of no more than eighty-seven pages, but worth more than many books of greater bulk on the same theme – the very title which he chose for it, *This Life and the Next*, links Thoreau's two worlds together and suggests that, like John, he believed that 'eternal life' is something which we may experience in foretaste even here and now, even if its consummation lies otherwise.

In his literary testament Forsyth therefore not only sets down his thought on the next life as Christians ought to conceive it, but strongly stresses the effect on this life of belief in another and better one beyond death. It is a theme as old as I Cor. 15 where the apostle whom Forsyth called 'the fifth evangelist' bids his readers consider what follows 'if Easter is not true' and then goes on to show how belief in a risen and regnant Christ ought to colour and shape our life and conduct here and now.

To be sure, Forsyth does not argue his case precisely as Paul did with the Corinthians, but his belief in the reality of Christ's triumph over 'the last enemy', death, is as firm as the apostle's, and he is as sure that our Christian experience in this life – our consciousness of being forgiven and regenerated by God's grace through the cross and by the power of the Holy Spirit at work in us – helps us to understand the nature of the life here-after and ought to shape the life we now live in the flesh.

Let us try to pick out and comment on the main themes of a book which sets forth the richness of the Christian hope with a quite lovely simplicity.

In our day critics of the faith are not slow to write off the Christian hope as so much 'pie in the sky when you die' and to dismiss Christianity as a creed which teaches men to fix their eyes on another world when they ought to be rolling up their sleeves to tackle the problems and tragedies of this one. The charge, in other words, is that the Christian hope is egoistic – purely selfish and self-regarding – and that it is a way of escape from the miseries of earth.

Forsyth is quick to answer this criticism. He does not deny that the Christian hope has often been so presented by Christian preachers. Egoist such preaching becomes, he says, if it portrays the great hereafter as 'an immortality of the *élite* or if it 'sets people elbowing each other out of the way to get at the elixir of eternity'. But all this is a grotesque travesty of the Christian truth. For, if God is an egoist, his is an egoism like that of which Augustine wrote: 'Thou hast made us for thyself', as God's seeking of his own in the saving work of Christ was for a world's blessing and reconciliation. No, 'the Christian ground for immortality is that the Lord hath need of him'.[1]

What can be called egoistic, says Forsyth, is the cult of spiritualism. Which is healthier, he asks, to put your dear departed in God's hands and pray for them, or to use strange devices in an attempt, like King Saul's at Endor, to conjure them up from the dead?

Having cleared the Christian hope from the slur of egoism, Forsyth makes the first of three great affirmations about it: 'The other life then is the other life now.'[2] Eternity is not simply something which supervenes when time is no more; eternity pervades time:

> The drift of pinions, would we hearken,
> Beats at our own clay-shuttered doors.

Therefore even in this life we may 'practise eternity', live on earth as those whose true home is in heaven. (Had not Paul said, 'We are a colony of heaven'?) Through fellowship with the living Christ who has redeemed us we may have proleptic experience of the eternal life of that God with whom is no before or after. And the secret of such fellowship lies in getting to know the only true God through his 'apostle' Jesus Christ (John 17.3), in a communion of person with person, spirit with spirit. 'Time,' says Forsyth, 'is a sacrament of eternity'; and to have part and lot here and now in God's eternity not only sets the tasks and tragedies of this life against the background of another, but should arm and inspire the humblest soul with hope and power.

So to affirmation No. 2: 'Immortality is a gift'[3] – the gift of God in Christ his Son. 'I do not remember,' observes our author, 'where we have Christian warrant for believing that man was created immortal.'[4] (The doctrine that the soul is naturally immortal and must survive the shock of death is Platonic, not Christian. Nowhere in the New Testament do we learn that we are, by our intrinsic nature, immortal beings.) Our hope of a blessed life hereafter rests wholly on the grace of the Father of our Lord Jesus Christ. The relation of sonship to God which was Christ's by nature becomes ours by his gift. We are 'adopted sons' (as Paul says); for it is in union with Christ that we become 'nurslings of immortality'. In truth, the life beyond is the continuance of that 'new birth' which once on earth set our life in another key than the natural. For if Christians die once, they are born twice.

If we wonder what life will be like hereafter, the clue is given us in Christ's own resurrection: 'It is not the resurrection of the flesh but of a body – not of matter but of form.'[5] (Just so Paul teaches in I Cor. 15.) What happens to our physical body, says Forsyth, is a matter of indifference to faith. (He does not say so explicitly, but he would obviously have had no difficulties, as some have, about cremation.) And when we die in union with Christ 'we pass into no lone immortality'. For 'we so worship here as worshipping with the greater part of the one church there'[6] – the church triumphant in the unseen world. As for the old debate about freewill, predestination and universalism, was the whole pith of the matter ever better expressed than by Forsyth: 'We are all predestined in love to life, sooner or later – if we will.'[7] It is the same answer as his Lord once gave in 'the days of his flesh'. Once someone asked Jesus, 'Sir, are only a few to be saved?' Jesus answered, 'Struggle to get in by the narrow door, for I tell you that many will try to enter and not be able' (Luke 13.23.) The question of theological curiosity is turned thus into what we would now call an existential challenge, a challenge in terms of personal decision and action. We have no key to the eternal destiny of others except that which we have to our own. So to the question, 'Are only a few to be saved?' Jesus' answer is (says Forsyth[8]): 'Few enough to make you fear you may not be there. See to your entry.'

But if this is how Forsyth would have us answer theological inquisitives, how are we to reply to those who remind us of all the piteous heart-aches of humanity, the failures and frustrations of our earthly lot, its unexplained sufferings, its unfulfilled hopes? This question Forsyth had already answered in Christian terms in the last chapter of *The Justification of God* – 'the conquest of time by eternity'. In *This Life and the Next* he sums it up in his third and last aphoristic affirmation: 'The future there is the fruition of failure here.'[9] It is the answer Browning had given in his *Abt Vogler*: 'On the earth the broken arcs, in the heaven a perfect round.' 'Time', says Forsyth, quoting William Blake, 'is the mercy of eternity.' It is here, by God's gracious appointing, to make eternity accessible to us. So the disciplines and disappointments of earth, so often hard for us to understand, are meant to bear a rich harvest hereafter. Eternity holds the key not only to the long travail of history but also to the interest of our tears. There is a region, he says, where the triumph of Christ's cross is realized as it is not here; and all the lesser crosses we have to bear on earth will there fructify, take on fresh meaning, stand in a new light:

> Heaven will the mysteries explain,
> And then sometime we'll understand.

'Eternal life', says Forsyth[10] 'is the enhancement and warrant of human joy and weal. It is the fixing of its finest colours. It is the last Amen.'

Thus, like Paul in writing to the Philippians, Forsyth links the Christian life here with the life hereafter. 'To live is Christ,' he says,[11] 'to die is more Christ.' Christian death is the only close which is more of a beginning than an end. We are not Moslems who hope hereafter to indulge afresh the egoist appetites of earth – 'only with better machinery there than here'. Not crude and carnal happiness of this sort but moral perfection is the end for which God designed us – that perfection which is the growth in us of God's image and glory – the image and glory we behold in Christ. (So Paul had described the Christian's destiny as a being 'shaped to the likeness of God's Son' and John had put the matter in five moving monosyllables: 'We shall be like him.')

Yet perhaps the most memorable thing Forsyth says[12] in his seraphic little book comes not in the last chapter but in its fourth where he is writing *De Mortuis* and commending prayers for the dead as Christian: 'There are those who can say, as their faith follows their love into the unseen, "I know that land. Some of my people live there. Some have gone abroad there on secret foreign service, which does not admit of communications. But I meet from time to time the Commanding Officer and when I mention them to Him, He assures me all is well." '

On this nobly Christian note let us end our exposition of Forsyth's theology.

Now, in closing our study of Forsyth, let us consider some of the criticisms that have been made of his theology, before briefly appraising it as a whole.

It has been said that you either swear with Forsyth or swear at him. By now it should be obvious in which camp the writer stands. Yet admirers of Forsyth are not absolved from the duty of looking squarely at some of the charges which have been levelled at him, in order to see whether they are fair and well founded.

That Forsyth dwelt too much on the holiness of God to the neglect of his love has been a common complaint. Yet if he never tired of telling his readers that God's was a holy love, was he not justified in so doing, and do we not still need to take his lesson to heart? 'Man's chief end is to glorify God', *The Shorter Catechism* had said. But modern man, elated by his mastery over nature and a belief in inevitable and irreversible progress, had come to think that God (if he believed in him at all) was there to serve him – to gratify the instincts and aspirations of the human heart. Not only had men grown 'pally with deity', but they had come to think of the holy Father above as someone to be 'used' rather than to be sanctified. More, they had so cheapened and sentimentalized that Father's love that it had become the mere superlative of romantic love. How far all this was away from the God of the Bible! How far away from 'the Father of an infinite majesty' invoked in that Lord's Prayer whose first petition reads, 'Hallowed be thy name!'

If then Forsyth peppered his pages with that old word 'holy', if he declared that holiness was not a mere attribute of God but his very nature, if he insisted that his love was not hearty but holy, did not his generation need to be rudely reminded that (as

Otto was about to remind them) the essence of religion lies not in knowledge or good conduct but in *awe* – our response to the *tremendum* of the Divine – and recalled to the true nature of God as he is portrayed in the Bible from Isaiah of Jerusalem to the seer of Patmos. 'In the midst of the rainbow there is a throne.'

Another objection has been at Forsyth's concentration on the cross to the alleged neglect of the life and teaching of Jesus. Here Forsyth is obviously reacting against the liberals of his day who played down the cross and played up the Sermon on the Mount, who regarded Christ primarily as teacher and not as saviour. Forsyth's reply[13] was: 'What makes Christ Christ is what he did as his life's crowning work; not how he was born or grew up, not even what he said and did from day to day – except as such words and deeds take their consummation and have their last meaning in his condensed word and summary work of the cross.' Has not the progress of critical scholarship since his day abundantly supported his contention? The finest modern account of the teaching of Jesus[14] as we have it in the Synoptic Gospels begins thus:

Historic Christianity is first and foremost a Gospel, the proclamation to the world of Jesus Christ and him crucified. For the primitive church the central thing is the Cross on the Hill rather than the Sermon on the Mount . . . Christian doctrine and Christian ethics may be the inevitable corollaries of the Christian Gospel; but they are corollaries. What is preached in the first instance is something that God has done for man in Christ. Only when this has been appropriated does the question arise how we are to think of the God who has done this great thing, or how we are to order our lives as Christians.

Again (and still on 'the cruciality of the cross'), some theologians have been unhappy about Forsyth's retention of the penal idea in his doctrine of atonement. They have rightly recoiled from the suggestion that God could have punished his well-beloved Son. But so too did Forsyth. Yet it is surely another matter to agree (as Forsyth did) that Christ in his obedience to God and in his compassion for men, consented (as we see him doing in Gethsemane and hear him in the cry of dereliction) on behalf of sinners to endure God's holy reaction to the sin of man and to enter the dark shadow of his penalty upon it.

Here two things may be said in favour of Forsyth. First, whether we like it or not, there is good evidence in the New Testament (and especially in Paul's letters) for holding that the sufferings of Christ were in some sense penal.[15] Second: great modern writers on the atonement – Denney, Mozley, Brunner and Vincent Taylor – are agreed that in any true account of Christ's saving work the penal element must find a place.

Once again, some have held that in his teaching about the sacraments Forsyth exalts the moral and disparages the mystical. So he does; but when we remember what magical notions men have imported into the sacraments, we may begin to understand why. Thus he repudiates the Catholic doctrine of transsubstantiation – the miracle by which 'a crumb of bread is under our eyes converted into the very body of Christ at the word of a man', while complaining[16] that some Protestants are so spiritually obtuse that they sing without a qualm Newman's famous words:

> And that a higher gift than grace
> Should flesh and blood refine,
> God's presence and his very self
> And essence all divine.

According to the New Testament, he reminds them, there is nothing higher than 'grace', which is the holy God hating sin and redeeming the sinner. 'God,' he says, 'is not more of himself in his essence (which we know nothing about) than in his grace (which we know intimately).'

Yet, this said, Forsyth prefers what he calls 'the lovely errors of the Mass' to a mere Zwinglian 'memorialism' since 'the theosophy of the Mass', in however magically mistaken a way, does keep the rite in close connection with the sacrifice of Christ and the virtue of the living Crucified who meets us in the sacrament. None the less, he reiterates, the real gift in the Lord's supper is forgiveness rather than food, regeneration rather than ecstasy.[17]

One modern writer dares to fault Forsyth for the lack of biblical exegesis in his books. The charge will not lie. Has he forgotten how again and again Forsyth stops to exegete a parable (like Dives and Lazarus or the Prodigal Son) or to draw out the capital importance of such a chapter as I Cor. 2 for a true doctrine of apostolic inspiration? But the true answer to this criticism is chapter 3 above where we have shown that the whole edifice of Forsyth's theology rests on a biblical scholarship which at point after point anticipates and reflects the best biblical insights of today.

The other criticisms made concern Forsyth's style (a matter discussed in chapter 2 above), the inconsistency sometimes found in his terminology, the unsystematic nature of some of his books, his failure to furnish them with indexes. On these points we need not hurry to his defence, save to say that generally he wrote at great speed to serve the need of the hour, never striving after that 'perfectionism' which makes some men write and re-write till they have corrected most of the sap and spring out of their work.

Somewhere Matthew Arnold supposes us challenging Shakespeare with this or that inconsistency or piece of fustian in his plays, and Shakespeare answering with a tolerant smile that no doubt we were right, but, after all, 'Did it greatly matter?' Just so we may imagine Forsyth candidly admitting that his books were often unsystematic and in passages unclear, but confining his apologia for such defects to the plea that, like Paul to the Galatians, he was writing for men who were in danger of 'resiling' from the grace of God as we have it in the New Testament.

A final short word of appraisal. 'Theology', said Forsyth, 'is faith thinking.' How effectively did Forsyth's faith explore the fact of Christ? Take his theology as a whole – consider his salutary accent on the holy majesty of God, the realism of his doctrine of man's sin and guilt, his focusing of the work of

Christ in the atoning cross, his Protestant but high concept of church and sacraments, his penetrating but practical discussion of the Christian ethic, his reading of the riddle of history and the world's goal in terms of the last judgment effected in principle on the cross, his deeply-spiritual reflections on this life and the next, and, perhaps above all, his doctrine of the person of Christ – and who will deny that here 'is a marrow of truly modern divinity' based on the gospel of God's grace in Christ which made both church and Bible, and withal ever trying to speak in contemporary terms to modern man.

In P. T. Forsyth we find a noble faith in the adequacy of the gospel, when set in modern idiom, to meet the need of sinful man not only in this time of the troubling of the nations and mankind's dread fear of nuclear holocaust but in every crisis when men cry out for a creed that will fortify them to face all life's tragedies and terrors. To make Forsyth's faith one's own is to believe that the key to history is the historic Christ, above history and in command of it, that the grace of God is the ground-work of the universe, and that the spinal cord of history is redemption.

NOTES

1. *TLTN*, p. 31.
2. *Ibid*, p. 48.
3. *Ibid*, p. 68.
4. *Ibid*, p. 21.
5. *Ibid*, p. 77.
6. *Ibid*, p. 78.
7. *Ibid*. p. 16.
8. *JOG*, p. 65.
9. *TLTN*, p. 80.
10. *Ibid*, p. 86.
11. *Ibid*, p. 84.
12. *Ibid*, p. 37.

13. *C. and S.*, p. 30.
14. T. W. Manson, *The Sayings of Jesus*, SCM Press 1949, p. 9.
15. See R. G. Crawford's article, 'Is the penal theory of the Atonement scriptural?' in *Scottish Journal of Theology*, August 1970.
16. *C. and S.*, pp. 37, 273.
17. *Ibid*, p. 279.